TENNESSEE STATE SYMBOLS

The fascinating stories behind our flag and capitol,
the mockingbird, iris and other official emblems.

Rob Simbeck

Altheus Press
Nashville

Published by Altheus Press
   P.O. Box 25274
   Nashville, TN 37202-5274

These pieces first appeared in slightly different form in *The Tennessee Conservationist* magazine.

Cover design by Angie Jones, The Art Studio. Cover photographs: Ladybug, passionflower and iris by Terry Livingstone; flag and capitol by Tennessee Photographic Services; mockingbird by Harold Key; raccoon by Tennessee Department of Tourist Development. Back cover photo by Aubrey Watson.

[Note: Every effort has been made to locate the copyright owners of material reproduced in this book. Omissions brought to our attention will be corrected in subsequent editions.]

Publisher's Cataloging in Publication Data
Simbeck, Rob.
   Tennessee state symbols: the fascinating stories behind our flag and capitol, the mockingbird, iris and other official emblems / Rob Simbeck.
      p. cm.
   Includes bibliographical references and index.
   ISBN 0-9642991-8-6
      1. Tennessee—History—Miscellanea. 2. Almanacs, American—Tennessee. 3. Natural history—Tennessee. I. Title
F436.5.S56 1994   976.8
                  QBI94-2199

Library of Congress Catalog No. 94-079271
SAN 298-380X

Printed in the United States of America
5 4 3 2 1

To Debby, with love

Contents

Tennessee Department of Tourist Development

Tennessee's wild animal, the raccoon.

Acknowledgements

This book had its origins in a conversation I had with Valary Marks early in 1989. Valary was and is the very talented editor of *The Tennessee Conservationist*, and she had been looking for someone to write a series on our state symbols. I jumped at the assignment, figuring we probably had at least five or six, giving me ready-made stories for a year or more, since the magazine is bimonthly.

I had, of course, greatly underestimated the Tennessee

Legislature. There are currently 29 symbols, and it took us 19 articles to cover them all. The first, on the flag, appeared in the July-August 1989 issue of the *Conservationist*. The last (so far), on the zebra swallowtail butterfly, appeared in the September-October 1994 issue.

The process was nothing less than an adventure. I interviewed and got to know people all over Tennessee, dug around in the state archives, capitol and museum, haunted libraries, took to the forests, fields, lakes and streams, and had a great time doing all of it. I've developed an entirely new appreciation for the flora, fauna and rock underpinnings of the state, and for the people who study and work with them.

While the pieces ran, the *Conservationist* and I received a number of requests for copies of the entire series. Valary, in fact, mailed out some photocopied compilations. With that as impetus, I began planning this book.

I am indebted to many, many people. I would like to thank, first of all, the staffs of the State Library and Archives, the Ben West Branch of the Nashville/Davidson County Metropolitan Library and its Nashville Room, and the research library of *The Tennessean*.

Any number of teachers, businesspeople, public servants, and enthusiasts of one sort or another were generous with their time and knowledge, and they are in great measure responsible for the information in this book. Any errors, though, are mine, not theirs. Thanks to Dianne Neal, Evelyn Garrington, Ruby Martin and Eunice Golden in the Governor's Office; Carolyn Newman and Margaret Tolleson in the Secretary of State's office; Malina Hudson in the Treasurer's Office; Deb Stutz, the Senate's Chief Engrossing Clerk; Secretary of State Riley C. Darnell and the people who compile the *Tennessee Blue Book*; Don Wick, Mark Goodlin, Robert Todd and the other staffers of the Tennessee Wildlife Resources Agency; the staffs of the Ellington Agricultural Center and the state's Geology Department; Jim Hoobler of the Tennessee State Museum; Dale Conner of J. T. Lovell;

John Latendresse; Kenneth Greene; Mrs. Wilbur ("Miss Jenny") Vaughan; Mrs. Elaine Baggett; Dr. Jamie Yanes; Dr. Paris Lambden; Michael Bierly; Debby Bowen; Mrs. Fred Blank; Gene Edwards; and Cheryl Karolchik. Thanks also to Patsy Weiler for timely support and encouragement.

Many of these stories were written at Wolfestone Typesetting, where I used to work, and I'd like to thank Kathy, Tom, Nola, Linda, Ron and Frances for their help and friendship. Thanks to Harold Fann for his assistance and computer wizardry. Special thanks go to my friend Ron Stone. It would be hard to overstate the help he gave me in preparing the book for publication.

Thanks to the photographers who have so generously contributed to this work: Aubrey Watson, Terry Livingstone, Vernon Summerlin, Harold Key and Russell Bromby; American Pearl Company; Dave Murrian of the Tennessee Wildlife Resources Agency; Tennessee Photographic Services; the Tennessee Department of Tourist Development, particularly Jed DeKalb and Murray Lee; the U.S. Fish and Wildlife Service; the Library of Congress and the Tennessee State Library and Archives. Many thanks also to Mary Skinner and Angie Jones for their artistry.

Sincere thanks go to Valary Marks for her guidance, her review of the pieces, her sweet disposition and her continued friendship, and to J. Michael Dolan for friendship and guidance throughout the process that led to this book.

I owe a special debt of gratitude to Kuni, Lyle, Leo, Grandma, Dick and Donna, Ethel, Wiggy and Tinch, who have always shared themselves, their knowledge, their guidance and their love. Thanks, too, to Bobbie Beasley, Frank Donnelly, Eric Bettelli and Barbara Yontz for love, friendship and support beyond the call of duty.

Finally, and most importantly, I would like to thank my parents, Bob and Kathleen, who taught me to love learning and to follow my own path, and my sisters, Karleen and Lori, who have always encouraged and been there for me.

One of many species of ladybug—in this case, the convergent ladybird beetle—one of Tennessee's state insects.

Introduction

There was a time when the only symbol Tennessee had was a borrowed seal. Although the state's 1796 Constitution called for a state seal, which was to be used to authenticate records and papers, Tennessee's first two governors, John Sevier and Archibald Roane, had to use their personal seals for a total of six years, until the state had one made. Finally, on April 24, 1802, Tennessee received its official seal, and we had our first state symbol.

As of this printing, we have 29—the seal, the flag, the capitol, eight songs and a poem, four insects, two birds, a mammal, two fish, two flowers, two trees, two gems, a rock and a folk dance. They are "official" because, with the exception of one state song, they have been the result of legislative action. This book is a celebration of those symbols, a close look at the natural and manufactured items Tennesseans see as emblematic of their collective heritage.

Symbols predate history. From the first time a heartsick human, missing home and loved ones, heard the song of a bird or caught sight of a flower that brought back memories and emotions, the symbol—something that stands for or suggests something else—has been with us. Cave drawings of game animals symbolized the hunt and kept its memory and its glory alive. The reality of power and authority could also be suggested: the Sumerians, Assyrians and Babylonians used seals to symbolize the officials behind documents. Medieval heraldry grew out of the use of identification marks on shields. The totem poles of Northwest American Indians and the Japanese *mon*, or crest, help speak of the universality of symbolism.

The combination of official and nostalgic symbol is evident everywhere in the United States. The flag, the Great Seal, the Statue of Liberty and the bald eagle have become shorthand for ideals, for power, for pride, for unity. They are rallying points, psychic markers.

Tennessee's wealth of symbols speaks alternately of its principles, its unity, its natural beauty and its cultural and commercial heritage. Some, like the capitol, denote strength and idealism; others, like the iris or the mockingbird, are essentially nostalgic rallying points—the formal, state-level equivalent of a loved-one's handkerchief or photograph, something to stir the heart or jog the emotions. There are unofficial symbols, things associated in an emotional way with the state—Graceland, Opryland, the Ryman Auditorium, the new Chattanooga aquarium, the Smokies—but since they have never received official legislative sanction, they are out-side the scope of this book.

Every state has symbols. Many—flag, bird, tree—are common to all, but there are a number of symbols even Tennessee, with its more than two dozen, hasn't considered. Alabama, for instance, has a reptile and a shell; Kentucky has state colors; Virginia has a dog, a fossil and a shell; and North Carolina has a historic boat and a beverage.

Given its current wealth of symbols, Tennessee was rather dilatory in kicking off the process. There was no real haste in settling on a permanent capital or picking a flag, for instance. The former didn't happen until 1845, the latter until 1905. Many states selected symbols of various kinds before Tennessee chose its next, the passionflower, in 1919. In fact, all but 10 states had by that time chosen a state flower. The first of our many state songs—"Tennessee," by A. J. Holt—was actually chosen by the organizers of the state centennial celebration in 1897 but was never adopted by the Legislature. The first to have that honor was "My Homeland, Tennessee," in 1925.

In 1933, the Legislature chose the mockingbird as state bird and the iris as a second state flower (setting off a brouhaha that wasn't officially settled until 1973); in 1935, it chose "When It's Iris Time In Tennessee" as another official song; in 1947, the tulip poplar as state tree; in 1955, "My Tennessee" as official state public school song; in 1965, "Tennessee Waltz" as another song; in 1969, agate as state rock; in 1971, the raccoon as state animal; in 1973, "Oh Tennessee, My Tennessee" as state poem; in 1975, the firefly and ladybug as state insects, and "The Tennessee Salute" as a state bicentennial song; in 1976, "Fly, Eagle, Fly" as another state bicentennial song; in 1979, the freshwater pearl as state gem and limestone as state rock; in 1980, the square dance as state folk dance; in 1982, "Rocky Top" as the (so far) final state song; in 1987, the bobwhite quail as state game bird; in 1988, the channel catfish and largemouth bass as state fish; in

1990, the honeybee as state agricultural insect; and in 1994, the zebra swallowtail as butterfly.

The natural world is obviously well-represented in this group, something consistent with Tennessee's renowned outdoor splendor. The plants and animals selected can, in fact, provide us with an unofficial but telling statement about the state's impact on the land's bounty. It is a decidedly mixed record.

The extensive forest-clearing associated with the state's settlement seems to have been good for mockingbirds and fireflies. Mockingbirds, in fact, are thought to be more abundant now than when Columbus landed. They thrive in association with humans. Fireflies, likewise, are more suited to fields and yards than to forests.

Ladybugs, natural predators of the insects that feed on food crops, have been pushed aside by pesticides, which have no doubt reduced their numbers greatly. In some parts of the country, they are being reintroduced as natural pesticides, but that practice is still in its infancy. Runoff from the use of those chemicals has been a longtime contributor to a reduction in the number of mussels that produce freshwater pearls. After devastating reductions in their population by overharvesting at the hands of people looking for pearls, man-made pollutants from agricultural, municipal and industrial sources have added further impediments to their survival. The invasion of the zebra mussel bodes poorly for native species as well. Channel catfish and largemouth bass are hardy species that are, nevertheless, affected by pollution, water levels, the health of aquatic grasses, and so on. Catch-and-release programs among fishermen have helped bass populations in recent years.

Farming activities have also had a major impact on the bobwhite quail, since these game birds prefer weedy pockets and wide fencerows. Perhaps 20 percent of their habitat has been lost to suburban sprawl in the past 25 years. The weedy edges needed by bobwhite quail have also been the home of the passionflower, which has long been fought as a pesky weed by farmers and gardeners alike.

The raccoon, an adaptable and intelligent mammal, faced severe pressure when its coat was in vogue in the 1920s and, to a lesser degree, when coonskin caps were fashionable in the '50s, but it has rebounded.

We may never see stands of tulip poplar trees like those that greeted early settlers here. Specimens almost 200 feet tall and 33 feet around near the base flourished. Logging eventually took nearly all of the virgin stand, and those remaining are much smaller.

Finally, the honeybee in one sense lies essentially outside the scope of such an overview, since it is not native to Tennessee—or to America; it was brought by European settlers. Still, it is in the midst of a telling environmental drama. Tracheal mites, which can cause honeybees to suffocate and which first appeared in the state in 1987, affect more than half of the hives in the state, and cutbacks in the number of state inspectors have raised concerns. Then, there is the continued approach of Africanized (killer) bees, which could interbreed with honeybees here—provided they can stand our winters.

The case of the honeybee brings up the fact that the motivation behind a move to name a state symbol can be very practical. It did not escape those behind the push for the honeybee as state agricultural insect that if and when killer bees get here, or should mites prove a particularly devastating problem, state funds may be necessary. If they are, perhaps the fact that the honeybee is a state symbol will be advantageous. A similar case can, of course, be made for the bobwhite quail. Mussels have faced daunting challenges too, though, and there is no real indication that its status as a symbol has helped.

Undoubtedly there will be more symbols suggested by citizens, introduced and debated by legislators, then passed into law. Since it's bound to happen anyway, I'd like to start the ball rolling. Tennessee is blessed with both wild and domesticated berries, with blackberries and blueberries calling Tennessee summers to mind with special poignancy. How about making one official? Maybe there are some students out there who'd like to do a little research—very tasty research, in this case—and start the process again. If it happens, be sure to give me a call.

Flag

It was the last day of February, 1885. Grover Cleveland would be sworn in as the nation's 22nd president in four days, and William B. Bate, governor of Tennessee, was breathing a huge sigh of relief. He had been scrambling to find a state flag to send to Washington for use on inauguration day, and it was finally in his hands.

In an apologetic letter to Colonel A. A. Nixon, he wrote, "We had to have the flag made and only got it finished and

Tennessee Photographic Services

Raising the flag over the capitol.

delivered to us yesterday evening." Because time was short, the letter—and the flag—were hand-delivered.

It's uncertain how many times similar scenarios were played out, but for 100 years following its 1796 admission to the Union, Tennessee had no official flag. Unofficial banners, "usually variations on the Stars and Stripes," according to historian Robert McBride, were flown at functions requiring them. An 1886 letter describes the state flag—possibly the same one shipped so hurriedly to Washington the year before—as bearing the Tennessee coat of arms encircled by an oak wreath.

The Tennessee Centennial Exposition of 1897, held in Nashville and featuring as its centerpiece a re-creation of the Parthenon, was apparently the spur for the first official state flag. In another last-minute gesture, the Legislature approved a new banner on April 30. Governor Robert L. Taylor signed the bill into law as the exposition was opening on May 1.

Photographs of the exposition show what is probably that flag flying with the Stars and Stripes, but the Legislature never called for its manufacture or distribution, and it was notable chiefly for the lack of public enthusiasm it generated. The reason, according to McBride, was aesthetic. "It is not a good design," he wrote.

In fact, the flag is a rather awkward-looking affair with three diagonal bands representing faithfully but clumsily the state's geographic divisions—East, Middle and West. The words "The Volunteer State" appear in the center band, and the number "16"—Tennessee was the 16th state admitted to the Union—appears on the right.

It wasn't until 1905 that the state settled on the flag currently in use. We owe its design to Captain LeRoy Reeves, a young Johnson City lawyer who organized and headed Company F of the Tennessee National Guard's Third Regiment. His flag also incorporates the state's three divisions, but his handling of them was a major improvement.

"The stars are of a pure white," he wrote, "representing the three grand divisions of the state. They are bound together by the endless circle of the blue field, the symbol being three bound together in one—an indissoluble trinity."

The white and blue stripes on the free end of the flag have no symbolic value and are there for reasons of design. "The final blue bar relieves the sameness of the crimson field and prevents the flag from showing too much crimson when hanging limp," Reeves stated. "The white edgings contrast more strongly the other colors."

Reeves himself wrote the bill, which set out in meticulous detail the flag's dimensions and specifications. It met unexpected (and unexplained) opposition from state Adjutant General Harvey H. Hannah, and it took some political sleight-of-hand to get it adopted. State Representative Walter Faw, former mayor of Johnson City, got House Speaker W. K. Abernathy to recognize him toward the end of the last day of the legislative session, and the measure slipped through.

Tennessee Department of Tourist Development

Governor John I. Cox signed the bill on April 17.

The flag's first use was, fittingly, over Reeves' own Company F. That flag is now in storage at the Tennessee State Museum.

In 1909, the General Assembly appropriated money for the purchase of two flags—one for the inside of the capitol and one for the outside—and the state finally had a flag it was flying officially.

Tennesseans as a whole, though, did not embrace the new banner overwhelmingly. In 1938, state information director Dr. Willis Boyd was so disheartened by lack of statewide interest in the flag that he started a drive to make Tennesseans flag-conscious.

Reeves' very specific instructions on how it should look did not prevent the most notorious slip-up involving the flag. In 1976, as part of the national Bicentennial celebration, the U.S. Post Office issued stamps displaying state flags. About half a million of those bearing Tennessee's flag were issued in Nashville to much fanfare, but a sharp-eyed state employee discovered that the flag on the stamp was flying upside down and backwards. The *Nashville Banner* reported that the post-master called the adjutant general just to be sure, then changed the flag in his own office. It was upside down. A quick check of the governor's information office disclosed that the flags it was selling were wrong too.

On the brighter side, the flag has inspired a good deal of old-fashioned patriotism. One-time state librarian John Trotwood Moore's poem on the flag [see next page] is widely reproduced, and the flag has a salute, written by Miss John Bostick [sic] of Franklin after she attended "Homecoming '86" festivities: "Flag of Tennessee, I salute thee. To thee I pledge my allegiance with my affection, my service and my life."

Its acceptance has grown, and over the years Tennesseans have carried their flag with them to remote corners of the earth.

THE FLAG OF TENNESSEE

Three stars upon a sky of blue,
A snow-white circle 'round;
Three Grand Divisions strong and true
By kinship's circle bound:
And one is East, and one is West,
And one is Middle ground.

Three stars within a circle white
Upon a crimson field,
Three hero-stars that led the fight,
Their souls with Courage steel'd:
And one was Jackson's, one was Polk's,
And one was Johnson's Shield.

The circle is for Unity,
The blue, its lofty aim;
The white stars are for purity,
The red field is their fame.
They rose above King's Mountain heights,
At New Orleans they led,
From Mexico to Flanders' Field
They guard our hero-dead.

Three stars upon a field of blue,
God keep them strong and free—
One stands for me, one stands for you,
One stands for Tennessee.

—*John Trotwood Moore*

Capitol

In 1845, William Strickland, one of America's foremost architects, told the Tennessee Legislature he could build a suitably grand state capitol in three years for $300,000—less if prison labor were used. Fifteen years and a million dollars later, the building's interior was incomplete, stones for the surrounding wall were piled haphazardly on the muddy grounds, the acoustics were terrible, and the roof was about to start leaking. To top it off, war with the North was imminent and the ground floor was being turned into an armory.

Amazingly enough, though, Tennesseans have the same highly functional and elegant state capitol 130 years later. The roof still leaks now and then, but a long and sometimes chaotic process of planning, construction, use and restoration has given us a lasting monument rich in both grandeur and in history.

As the 1840s dawned, Tennessee, which became a state in 1796, still didn't have a permanent capital. The state was looking for one, though, and Nashville was vying for the honor. To sweeten the pot, the city threw in its most prominent hill, which offered a commanding view of the area. It got the nod.

The Capitol Commission called on Strickland, a Philadelphian who had designed the Bank of the United States and the Philadelphia Exchange. A patrician man of wide-ranging interests and talents, he agreed to design the capitol if he could supervise construction—for the then-tidy sum of $2,500 per year. He arrived in Nashville in May of 1845, a month before Andrew Jackson's death. In July, the capitol's cornerstone was laid.

The quarry was nearby, at Charlotte and 14th, and its proximity to the prison, at Church and 15th, was a major asset, since prison labor, as well as some slave labor, would be used. Most of the workers were craftsmen and laborers, who were paid from $1 to $2.50 per day.

The mixture was bound to create tension. In December 1845, disgruntled, out-of-work locals protested the use of prisoners, which free stonemasons never fully accepted either. The practice wasn't stopped, however, until years later when most of the stone had been quarried and rough-hewn.

Whatever its makeup, Strickland's work force did an incredible job. The stone blocks were so perfectly cut that the average mortar joint is less than three-sixteenths of an inch. Progress, though, was agonizingly slow. The Legislature doled out money in small portions, and there never seemed to be enough to work at the pace Strickland wanted. To finish a $300,000 job in three years, you'd need, of course, $100,000 per year. Instead, the total appropriation for 1846 and 1847 was $32,000. The amount was then increased to $50,000 per year, not enough to quicken the pace appreciably.

There were other annoyances as well. In 1847, Strickland complained about the sometimes obscene graffiti appearing on the walls, and the Assembly responded by making it a misdemeanor to "cut, write upon, deface, disfigure, or damage the state house."

In 1853, the price tag had reached $500,000, and while the building was not complete, the Legislature was able to meet inside it on October 3. Almost immediately, members complained of the echoes in its stone rooms. Draperies would help remedy that situation, but the condition of the building and grounds as a whole may be deduced from the fact that when Andrew Johnson was sworn in as governor just two weeks later, the capitol was deemed unsuitable for the event.

Johnson called for completion of the decade-old project and an end to the expenditure. The state was spending more and more, and Strickland's salary had become a sore point in some quarters. In February of 1854, the Legislature appropriated $200,000 with the understanding that it would finish the task. It didn't. One House member offered an alternate bill which reduced the figure to $10,000, saying that should complete it, whitewash it and put a good fence around it.

On April 7, 1854, Strickland died. He was entombed in a wall near the north entrance of the building, as he had requested, and nearly 3,000 people attended the ceremony. His son, Francis, took over his position at a much lower salary.

The last stone was laid in the tower on July 21, 1855, but the year of completion is commonly given as 1859, when the terrace was finished. Even then, there was much work to be done both inside and outside. A *Nashville City and Business Directory* from the early 1860s says, "The grounds, which are unenclosed, are in a most chaotic state, a mere mass of huge broken rocks, together with various dilapidated out houses, altogether a disgrace to the State and city."

Library of Congress. Copied for the James Hoobler Collection, Tennessee State Library and Archives.

Cotton bales and wooden palisades surround the unfinished state capitol, pressed into service as Fort Andrew Johnson during the Civil War. Building stones lie in the foreground. The cupola served as a lookout post, and it was there that Governor Johnson and his aides watched the Battle of Nashville. Many union soliders watched the battle from the adjacent grounds.

With the outbreak of war and Tennessee's secession in June 1861, work stopped and stones lay piled in the street, but the building was offered as the capitol of the Confederacy. In fact, it appeared on the first Confederate $20 bill.

In February 1862, Ulysses Grant took Fort Henry and then Fort Donelson, just 60 miles northwest of Nashville. On the 16th, in what became known as The Great Panic, Nashville was evacuated, with Confederate soldiers, the Legislature and the governor all moving to Memphis. The state's archives were loaded onto a train and taken as well. Two weeks later, Nashville became the first Southern capital to fall, as 10,000 Union soldiers entered the city. Like any other tourists, they flocked to see the new capitol, which was soon back in use, serving as the seat of government for former Governor Johnson, who was appointed military governor on March 3. Crude stockades were built, an artillery platform was dug out near the east steps, and soon the site was known as Fort Andrew Johnson. Its cupola served as a lookout post, and during the Battle of Stones River, from New Year's Eve to January 2, 1863, the capitol was used as a federal hospital. Late in the war, during the Battle of Nashville, the governor and his aides watched from the cupola as George H. Thomas' troops successfully defended the city from an army under John B. Hood. Union soldiers not engaged in combat joined a large gallery of spectators on the grounds during the battle.

After the war, the capitol superintendent reported that the roof leaked, the lightning rod was broken, windows were warped and couldn't be closed, gas pipes leaked, and stones in the floor of the House chamber were loose. Work on the grounds commenced in 1870, and progress was slow on the rest. It wasn't until 1885 that the roof was replaced.

There were other problems as well. The big building was heated with basement fires and hot air flues. Because these were ineffective, the Legislature moved its meetings from January to October. Even with pot-bellied stoves, the capitol remained a cold, damp place.

Probably the building's most famous flaw, though, is a chip in the marble of its main stairway. The damage occurred during debate over the 14th Amendment, which, among other things, granted citizenship, voting rights and due process to blacks. The state had to ratify the measure to be readmitted to the Union, and Rebels in the Legislature were determined to block that outcome. In order to prevent a quorum, several of them left for Kentucky. The sergeant-at-arms tracked them down, brought them back and locked them in a visitors' room. He apparently didn't lock them up well enough, though, because they broke out. As they were running down the steps, the sergeant-at-arms stopped at the top and shot at them, with one bullet digging a chunk out of the railing. They went back, a quorum was declared, the vote was taken, and Tennessee was readmitted.

The capitol has remained at the center of the state's political history in the 130 years since then, and the building and Tennessee State Museum are filled with reminders of our rich heritage. It endures as a potent symbol of the Volunteer State, although given the recent proliferation of imposing buildings in downtown Nashville, it no longer dominates the skyline the way it once did. Still, it remains a commanding presence from the city's northern and western approaches. It is by far our grandest state symbol, representing architecturally the stature, strength and durability of Tennessee's history, people, and way of life.

Built to house all three branches of state government, the capitol is a striking showpiece of the Greek Revival in architecture that flourished during the middle of the 19th century, and it remains a recognized masterwork by Strickland, one of the period's brightest lights.

Set on an 11-acre site comprising the highest point in downtown Nashville, the capitol is home to both the House and Senate chambers, the governor's office, and a number of other offices. Originally, the Supreme Court and State Library and Archives were housed there as well. The Supreme Court chamber was remodeled into offices when that body moved across Seventh Avenue North in 1937, but the chamber has since been restored to its original appearance. When, in 1954, the library was moved, also across the street, its former site was turned into the legislative lounge.

Four people are buried on the grounds, two of those in the walls of the building itself. President James K. and Sarah Polk lie near the east side of the building, where their remains were moved from their nearby home in 1893. While Strickland is buried in the wall near the north entrance, Samuel Dold Morgan, chairman of the commissioners who oversaw the project, is entombed near the south entrance.

The building, modeled after a Greek Ionic temple, is 238 feet long and 109 feet wide and has two 17-foot flagstone terraces surrounding it. The porticoes, modeled after those of the Erectheum, a temple to Athena built near the Parthenon on the Acropolis in the fifth century B.C., feature eight Ionic columns running the length of the north and south facades, and six at the east and west entrances. The columns are 33' 5" high and 4' 6" in diameter at the base.

The Bigby limestone that originally comprised most of the building was obtained less than a mile away at a quarry bounded by Charlotte Avenue, Pearl Street, and 14th and 15th Avenues. Strickland and others raved about the quality of the stone at the time, but their enthusiasm was premature. The limestone had seams of phosphate that were susceptible to the deleterious effects of moisture, and it was laid perpendicular to its natural state, heightening the destruction of time and weather. By the middle of the 20th century, large chunks of the stone were falling from the walls. During a major restoration between 1956 and 1958, 90,000 cubic feet of Indiana limestone were brought in to replace the original. The "marble" used in facings, actually polished, high-quality limestone, was quarried in East Tennessee. The other materials, from the wood used for doors, windows and roof sheathing to much of the iron work, were also obtained in-state.

The building's striking tower and cupola, or lantern, rise 79' 2" over the roof. They were modeled after the choragic Monument of Lysicrates, built in Athens in 335 B.C. to house a trophy won by a stage choir led by Lysicrates. The tower itself is 36' square and 42' high, with a window in each side. Above it lies the lantern, 26' 8" in diameter and 37' high, with eight Corinthian columns topped with elaborate capitals. There are 312 steps leading from the second floor to the top of the cupola.

The tower is a rarity among state capitols, 40 of which have domes. Strickland had used a similar tower, though, in another of his major works, the Philadelphia Exchange. The roof from which it rises was made originally of copper, but because inadequate allowance was made for expansion, it was quickly riddled with leaks. It was replaced in 1885, and finally re-done with copper in 1956.

The building was designed with central heat (a large fire in the basement and flues to various rooms) and indoor toilets, and it had a water collection system featuring eight-inch cast-iron gutter pipes that ran through the walls into basins under the terraces. The basement, an 18-foot substory, has been excavated to provide a good deal of office space that was not part of the original plan. The governor's communications, scheduling, correspondence and legislative offices are among those housed there. Excavation also provided a pedestrian tunnel and elevator, opened in 1958 to make the building much more easily accessible. Legislators and others had long complained of the climb up the hill to the building.

Although the south entrance has come into common use as the main entrance, that role was originally planned for the east entrance, above Sixth Avenue. Inside that door, in a foyer containing an information booth, are portraits of Tennessee's three U.S. presidents—Andrew Jackson, James K. Polk and Andrew Johnson—along with those of Strickland and Morgan. Nearby are several overhead frescoes by two German painters, Knoch and Schliecher, who also painted the library ceiling. They depict the Four Arts (painting, literature, sculpture, music), the state's Great Seal, Tennessee's "Western Frontier," Justice, Liberty and the American eagle.

The north-south hallway is lined with the portraits of past governors, from Joseph McMinn, elected in 1815, to Ned Ray McWherter, who left office in 1995, with notable Tennessee names like Trousdale, Cannon and Brown in between.

The first floor features the offices of the Comptroller, State Treasurer, Secretary of State and Commissioner of Finance and Administration. The showpiece among the

Library of Congress. Copied for the James Hoobler Collection, Tennessee State Library and Archives.

Soldiers' tents and cannons on the grounds of the Tennessee state capitol in 1864 during the Civil War. The statues and lampposts shown have long since been removed.

offices, though, is that of the governor. Its reception room features 11 panels painted in 1938 tracing the history of the state, furnishings that include an Empire sofa, Rococo parlor table and chairs, and the die of the State Seal.

The Supreme Court chamber down the hall is now home to several portraits, including those of a number of antebellum Tennessee justices.

The wide principal stairway near the west entrance leads to a landing, then doubles back on both sides to the second floor. Its marble balustrade is similar to those in the nation's Capitol, for which Strickland did work as an apprentice. Up the stairs are busts of Jackson, Polk and Johnson, and of Confederate General Nathan Bedford Forrest, Union Admiral David G. Farragut, oceanographer Matthew Maury, and John Sevier, Tennessee's first governor.

Aubrey Watson

The capitol rises behind Civil War hero Sam Davis, one of several people honored with statues and monuments on the capitol grounds.

On the ceiling overhead, below the building's tower, is a large gasolier, one of four originals still hanging in the capitol. A gasolier of similar proportion, with metal symbols of Tennessee—Indians, corn, buffalo, tobacco and cotton—once hung in the chamber of the House of Representatives. It so unnerved the Shelby County delegation, which sat directly below it, though, that its members were successful in getting it removed in 1889.

The chamber itself, at the south end of the floor, has a 42' ceiling, supported by 16 22' fluted Ionic columns, each made from one piece of limestone. At 100'x70', it is nearly three times as large as the Senate chamber down the hall. The latter is 70'x35', with a 43' ceiling and a 12'-wide gallery on three sides supported by 12 Tennessee red marble columns. Surrounding the House chamber are various clerks' offices, and above them, behind the columns, are visitors' galleries.

Across the hall from the Senate are the legislative lounge and the offices of the Speaker of the House and Speaker of the Senate. The lounge, formerly the library, boasts a cast-iron spiral staircase shipped from Philadelphia and embedded with white cameo portraits of great literary and historical figures. There are also portraits of governors and other prominent figures lining the walls and ceiling.

The capitol grounds have only slowly developed into their present form. For many years following construction, they remained unimproved. The first landscaping was done in the 1870s, and the latest major change was made in the early 1960s, with the addition of a new access road from Seventh Avenue, new parking and 600 trees.

The grounds' most distinctive feature is probably Clark Mills' equestrian statue of Andrew Jackson, located near the east entrance. It was unveiled before 30,000 people during an 1880 ceremony that was part of the celebration of the centennial of the founding of Nashville. Replicas stand in Washington, D.C., and New Orleans.

To the north of the statue lies Polk's tomb, which was also designed by Strickland, and to the south is a Masonic time capsule, to be opened in 2027. Farther south, near the corner of Charlotte and Sixth, is a statue of World War I hero Sergeant Alvin C. York. Legislator/journalist Edward Carmack, who was known for his "Pledge to the South," and who was shot to death on a Nashville street in 1908, is the subject of a statue in front of the south entrance. Young Civil War hero Sam Davis is similarly honored near the corner of Charlotte and Seventh.

While it has undergone a good deal of restoration and change, the capitol has fulfilled Strickland's original vision as a monument to the people and ideals of Tennessee. Its future as a Tennessee symbol seems as solid as the limestone bedrock it stands on, and its structural integrity has been verified. John Mesick, an Albany, N.Y., architect who did a historic structure report and provided the specifications for the latest round of remodeling, told the *Nashville Banner* in 1987, "If they can keep the roof good and tight, this place ought to be here for another thousand years or so."

Bird: Mockingbird

Just sitting there, a mockingbird is pretty uninspiring. It's a drab, grey bird with only one interesting feature—a long tail it sometimes holds at a rakish angle.

But as anybody who's seen one can tell you, a mockingbird hardly *ever* just sits there, and in flight or in song, this scrappy, noisy character looks and sounds like a natural choice for Tennessee's state bird.

There's no mistaking a mockingbird in motion. It's got

big splashes of white on its wings and tail that turn it from dull to spectacular, and it flashes those wings in courtship and territorial displays that look like a cross between sparring and dancing. Even when it's singing, perched high on a tree limb, TV antenna or telephone pole, it will periodically leap skyward, flapping and spiraling madly, then settle back onto its perch without missing a note. And when it sings, it does so in what is generally considered the most spectacular voice in the bird world, a voice that has earned the mockingbird its place as one of the enduring emblems of the South.

"The mockingbird stands unrivaled," wrote New England bird authority Edward Forbush. "He is the king of song. He equals and excels the whole feathered choir and improves upon most of the notes he reproduces."

No less a nature enthusiast than Theodore Roosevelt called the mockingbird "the most interesting of all feathered folk." While staying at a Maury County farm, Roosevelt was in a room that overlooked a moonlit magnolia featuring a mockingbird in the throes of night-long song.

"Sometimes he would perch motionless for many minutes," he wrote, "his body quivering and thrilling with the outpour of his music. Then he would drop softly from twig to twig, until the lowest limb was reached, when he would rise, fluttering and leaping through the branches, his song never ceasing for an instant, until he reached the summit of the trees and launched into the warm, scent-laden air, floating in spirals, with outspread wings, until, as if spent, he sank gently back into the tree and down through the branches, while his song rose into an ecstasy of ardor and passion."

It's not surprising that a bird that can inspire that sort of rapturous prose should be the state bird. Mississippi, Florida, Arkansas and Texas have also seen fit to adopt the mocker as a state symbol. In Tennessee, the matter was put to a statewide vote in 1933. Over 70,000 people cast ballots (about a third as many as voted in gubernatorial races at the time), and the mockingbird, with 15,553 votes, edged the robin, with 15,073. The cardinal, bobwhite and bluebird finished third through fifth.

Roosevelt was not the only presidential mockingbird fancier. Thomas Jefferson had a pet mockingbird he kept in his Washington study. It sat on his shoulder, picked food from his lips, and perched on the sofa during presidential naps. It would even follow him up the stairs, hopping step by step after him.

One Indian tribe called the mockingbird *cencontlatolly,* or "four hundred tongues" for its ability to imitate other species. That talent also gave the bird its scientific name, *Mimus polyglottos,* or "many-tongued mimic." It can mimic the song of just about any bird it's exposed to, and mockers have been known to imitate tree frogs, dogs, cats, hawks, crickets, injured chickens, sirens, alarm clocks, dinner bells, flutes and squeaking gate hinges, among other things.

Over the years, there have been debates in ornithological circles over how much of the mockingbird's song is borrowed. Some say anything that sings that much is going to sound like something else pretty often just by coincidence, and that less than 10 percent of its song involves imitation. Most, however, are convinced that much of what the mockingbird does is genuine mimicry. Dr. George Mayfield, writing in the *Nashville Tennessean* in 1933, said, "One individual located on Lebanon Pike near Mt. Olivet Cemetery (in Nashville) has a repertory of 38 species. Since there are only about 50 species of birds in this section classified as singing birds, you may see that he has a high percentage in his vocal powers."

The singing gets under way in late January and reaches a peak in spring, when unattached males will often sing all night, presumably in last-minute attempts to charm members of the opposite sex. It diminishes in late summer, then starts up again in the fall.

Because of their vocal talents, mockingbirds were sold as caged songbirds for many years, much as canaries are.

Federal law has long since prohibited the practice. Such episodes aside, mockingbirds are one of the few species that seem to thrive in contact with humans. It's thought that there

Harold Key

are more mockers in America now than when Europeans first landed here.

Their nests are usually near human habitation, three to 10 feet off the ground in thick shrubs, bushes or vines, or in dense trees like cedars. The male places nesting material in a couple of potential sites as part of his courtship ritual and the female picks one. Both take part in building the nest, and materials include twigs, grass, rootlets, bark strips, weed stalks, and sometimes string, moss, leaves, cotton, rags or paper.

The female lays one 1x¾-inch egg on each of three to five consecutive days, and incubates them for 12-13 days. During the two weeks the young stay in the nest, both parents feed them slugs, cabbage worms, cutworms, grubs, grasshoppers and crickets. Adults eat wild berries about half the time when they're available, supplementing their diet with beetles, caterpillars, spiders, snails, crawfish, sowbugs and lizards. At bird feeders, they've been known to eat suet, raisins, bread, berries, figs, apples, bananas and doughnuts.

The nestlings are vulnerable to a number of wild and domestic animals, and their mortality rate is high, but a mockingbird guarding a nesting territory is a force to be reckoned with. It will swoop down on and attack just about anything it feels threatened by, including owls and crows, snakes, squirrels and people. Dogs and cats have been known to be terrified to go out into their own yards because of constant attacks by mockers. A pair that set up a nest site near the state capitol in Nashville made newspaper headlines a few years back by attacking dozens of legislators and government employees walking to and from work.

In establishing those territories, mockingbirds will also fight each other, and dogfights involving up to 10 or 12 have been seen. During the winter, mates split up into separate feeding territories and show only marginal tolerance of each other.

With that many noisy and aggressive habits, the mockingbird can't help but draw attention to itself, and people have noticed. Statewide, Tennessee pays tribute to the mockingbird along its prettiest thoroughfares. There, on thousands of signs designating roads as "Tennessee Scenic Parkways," is a bigger-than-life reproduction of the showy bird that is one of our most vibrant state symbols.

Tennessee's state cultivated flower, the iris.

Flowers: Iris and Passionflower

Nowhere has Tennessee politics produced stranger bed-
fellows than in the flower bed. Two very dissimilar
species—the iris and the passionflower—have the
distinction of being the Volunteer State's official flowers.

The iris is an urban sophisticate with a long and glorious

history. It was treasured by the Egyptians 3,500 years ago and it has received the doting attention of Tennessee hybridizers and garden clubs. The passionflower, on the other hand, is a denizen of the forest trail or the edge of the cotton field. It's a creeping, tendrilled vine with an ostentatious bloom, and it was discovered by Europeans just a few hundred years ago. Both have had their adherents, and the process that got both recognized was not always a civil one.

Terry Livingstone
The iris.

That process began in 1919, when someone noticed that Tennessee was one of only 10 states without a state flower. Given that it took 100 years for Tennessee to adopt a flag, that wasn't surprising, but State Senator Andrew Todd and State Representative Seth Walker decided to do something about it. They sponsored a bill which said the state's schoolchildren should vote for a flower, which would then be adopted by the state as its own.

Kids being what they are, they overlooked millennia of horticultural effort and went straight to the woods and fields, to the passionflower, which is affectionately known as the maypop. The maypop's bloom, a showy purple and white flower, is followed by a two-inch green fruit you can stomp on to make a popping sound. When the fruit ripens and turns yellow, it can be eaten or used in making jelly [see recipe at end of chapter]. Such is the stuff summers were made of. The fruit was also responsible for the plant's other name, the wild apricot.

Some of the children probably knew the folklore surrounding the flower as well. Some species of passionflowers had first been spotted in South America by Spanish explorers and missionaries. They were claiming the continent for Christianity as well as for Spain, and everything about this flower shouted religious symbolism. Specifically, they saw symbols of the crucifixion of Christ. The five petals and five sepals represented the ten apostles traditionally thought to be present at the crucifixion. The three stigmas represented the nails driven into the hands and feet, and the five stamens were symbolic of the wounds to Christ's hands, feet and side. The curling tendrils recalled the scourges, the leaves were shaped like the piercing lance, and the fringed corona suggested the crown of thorns or a halo. This much symbolism in one place was taken as a sign that the missionaries were right in trying to convert the locals to Christianity.

Terry Livingstone

The Latin name for the genus, *passiflora*, comes from the words for passion and flower. It is one of the *The passionflower.* *Passifloracae* family's 12 genera containing 400 species, only seven of which, including the maypop (*Passiflora incarnata*) are native to the U.S.

A commission appointed by the Legislature counted the children's votes, published the results in the press and had State Librarian and Archivist John Trotwood Moore put out 10,000 copies of a pamphlet called, *Tennessee: State Flag-*

Flower-Song-Seal and Capitol, which announced the new state flower. Moore wrote a poem for the pamphlet [see page 15] bearing the Cherokee Indian name for the flower (*ocoee*), and reproduced a large illustration of it. He called the passionflower a "most fitting" selection.

That probably should have settled the matter, but it didn't. At about this time in Tennessee's history, with flower gardens growing in popularity, interest was developing in another showy spring bloomer.

The iris had been cultivated for thousands of years. Sixty genera and 800 species of the family *Iridaceae* were known, and it was the subject of widespread hybridization. It came in so many colors that its name was taken from the Greek goddess of the rainbow. King Thutmose III brought the iris to Egypt from Syria 1,500 years before Christ; it's represented on the walls of his temple at Karnak. Pliny gave detailed instructions for the ceremonial gathering of its roots, and it is the *fleur-de-lis* of French heraldry.

The Nashville Iris Association was formed in the early 1930s, and its efforts at breeding, growing and displaying irises had drawn both national and international attention to the city. Some, in fact, hoped the iris would do for Nashville tourism what the azalea had done for Charleston.

All of this interest in the iris eventually made it to the state Legislature. On April 22, 1933, it passed a bill that said, in part, "Whereas, The Iris is one of the most beautiful and one of the most popular flowers in the State, its profusion and beauty attracting many visitors to the State, Now, therefore, be it resolved...that the Iris be adopted as the State Flower of Tennessee."

What about the passionflower? Well, the bill opened with the following clause: "Whereas, The State of Tennessee has never adopted a State Flower...." It seemed as though everyone had forgotten the schoolchildren's vote 14 years earlier.

They hadn't. When the iris bill was made public, the uproar was incredible.

"We have all heard about the 'war of the roses,' " said the *Chattanooga News*, "but now it is our duty to give the latest communiques from the war of the iris and the passion-flower....It is reported now that the iris adherents only lift their eyebrows when the passionflower is mentioned, and bad blood is known to exist between the factions representing the two State flowers."

Newspapers statewide jumped into the fray, as did botanists and garden clubs. Much of what was said was tongue-in-cheek, but some were taking the matter as seriously as it could be taken.

"The iris, beautiful as it is, is too much a citizen of the world to be called the Tennessee state flower," said the *Knoxville News-Sentinel*. "And there are so many varieties of it you wonder which is ours." (While no variety or color has ever been specified, the *Tennessee Blue Book* says that "by common acceptance the purple iris is considered the state flower.")

"The Legislature did much better in its choice of a state bird [the mockingbird] by allowing the people of the state to express their preference," the *News-Sentinel* went on. "Since the Legislature unceremoniously 'kicked out' the passion-flower, why shouldn't it reopen the matter at the next session and let the people vote?"

Occasional salvos in the debate were fired as much as several years later. In 1939, the *Chattanooga News* reported that "Garden club presidents from various parts of the state, meeting in Chattanooga recently, adopted a resolution favoring the passionflower as Tennessee's State flower." After several paragraphs of background and floral partisanship, it concluded, "We are glad that the Garden Clubs recognize that the State Legislature of seventeen years ago had better taste in State flowers than the legislature of five years ago."

A Tennessee Garden Club convention just six months later, though, reversed the organization's earlier position, voting not to recommend that the state flower be changed from the iris to the passionflower, and passing up a chance to stir the whole matter up again in the Legislature.

Apparently no one thought to recognize both as state flowers. The *Nashville Banner* reported that, according to the secretary of state, the 1919 effort "was never carried through to a legislative conclusion." The *Blue Book* in 1942-43 said that "an opinion of the Attorney-General held that the iris is the official State flower."

As the furor died down, it became clear that the iris had indeed come into popular acceptance as the state flower. In 1935, "When It's Iris Time In Tennessee" was made an official state song. In 1949, then-governor Gordon Browning provided the nation's 47 other governors with purple Fords to drive during the National Governor's Conference in honor of the iris, and the *Blue Book* began mentioning the passionflower only as an antecedent to the iris.

It wasn't until 1973 that the matter again came to the attention of the Legislature. State Senator Edward Blank was being urged to introduce a bill to make the iris the state cultivated flower and the passionflower the state wildflower. Among those doing the urging was his mother, Mrs. Fred L. Blank, who was active in the Hampton Garden Club and the Tennessee Federation of Garden Clubs. Senator Blank mentioned both previous bills in introducing his bill in the Senate, and said, "The people of the good garden clubs across the state would like this resolved."

The Senate treated the measure with a light-heartedness that nearly escaped the House, which almost turned the bill into a major legislative imbroglio. Representative Tommy Powell of Memphis summed up early opposition to the measure: "I have never seen this [passion]flower, and the picture looks kind of funny to me. I don't much believe in buying any shoes 'til you try them on, and I just don't much want to vote on this until he [Senator Blank] brings some of these flowers in here and we take a look at them. If this thing's been going on since 1919, one more day ain't gonna hurt."

Arguments by Representative Edward Williams of Memphis and others that members of garden clubs had "besieged" them with support for the bill carried the day, and the final house vote was 89-1. The Senate vote had been 30-1.

Through all of this, the iris has remained a staple of gardens around the state, from front yards to botanical centers like Nashville's Cheekwood, which displays prize-winning varieties every spring.

The success of the passionflower is more problematic. It has become a pest in many soybean and cotton fields, its vines getting tangled in farm machinery. It has also been known to take over gardens planted near forests. Like the iris, though, the passionflower is represented at Cheekwood, in the wildflower garden.

And after a lot of fussing, Tennessee still has, at least for now, two quite different but decidedly beautiful state flowers.

Terry Livingstone

Maypop Jelly

Wash ripe yellow fruit thoroughly and slice enough to make 4 cups. Cover with water and boil gently in large saucepan (6- to 8-quart capacity) 10 minutes. Strain in jelly bag. Measure juice. Add enough water to make two cups total. Add ¼ teaspoon butter or margarine. Measure ⅓ package light fruit pectin and mix with ¼ cup sugar. Add to liquid and bring to a full rolling boil, stirring constantly. Quickly add 1¼ cup sugar and bring to another full rolling boil, stirring constantly. Boil for one minute, still stirring. Remove from heat. Skim off any foam with a metal spoon. Fill hot jars immediately to within ¼ inch of top. Cover with hot paraffin, then lid and band.

Ocoee: The Passionflower Poem

State librarian John Trotwood Moore, in the pamphlet *Tennessee: State Flag-Flower-Song-Seal and Capitol*, published the following poem with introduction in honor of the passionflower:

This beautiful flower, called by the early Spaniards the Passion Flower [sic], and by our own pioneers the May-Pop and Wild Apricot, was abundant all over Tennessee. The Cherokee Indians called it the Ocoee; hence the Ocoee valley and river; and they prized it as their most abundant and beautiful of all flowers. It is, therefore, most fitting that this flower be adopted as the State Flower.

OCOEE

"Oco-ee, Oco-ee, Oco-ee,"
The Indian maiden sang.
"Oco-ee, Oco-ee, Oco-ee,"
The echoing mountains rang:
"Give me thy blooms, Oco-ee,
Give me thy flowers rare,
Thy twilight blue of sunset hue
To bind my mourning hair.
Give me thy gems, Oco-ee,
Thy turquoise crown unfold,
Beset with bars of yellow stars
On calyxes of gold.
Oco-ee, once my bridal flower—
(Now widowed, thou shalt be,)
My warrior comes not home again,
He comes not home to me,
    Oco-ee."

"Oco-ee, Oco-ee, Oco-ee,
'Twas here he won my love,
Your flowers were my bridal bed
Blue as the skies above
Blue as the skies above
But oh, alas! he lies
Unburied in an unknown land
Beneath its unknown skies.
Thy gems are tears, Oco-ee,
(Ay, yellow tear forlorn!)
Thy blue is turned to ruth and rue
Thy turquoise crown is thorn.
Farewell, my land, my life, my love,
Farewell, oh flower of woe,
My warrior comes not home to me
But I to him will go,
        Oco-ee."

The flower and leaves of the tulip poplar tree.

Tree: Tulip Poplar

To the pioneers carving new lives out of the Tennessee Valley wilderness, there were few sights more welcome than a stand of tulip poplars. Where you had tulip poplars, you had good soil, so in clearing them you could expect to gain a fertile patch of farmland. Once you had cut them, the termite-resistant logs made for long-lasting cabins, and you could use the wood for lining your well, as flooring, and for odds and ends as diverse as silverware handles and musical instruments. In addition, game like squirrels and deer fed on the trees' fruit and twigs, and the bitter inner bark could be used as a tonic and stimulant.

Dwight Barnett/Tennessee Division of Forestry

The tall, straight trunks of a stand of 40-year-old tulip poplar in Carter County. The understory is primarily beech and hophornbeam.

This huge state symbol, chosen over contenders like the oak and hickory, has credentials that go deep into the region's history and economy. Daniel Boone was one of those who put the tree to a common pioneer use—when he left Kentucky with his family, he did so in a 60-foot canoe carved out of a single tulip poplar. The floor of Andy Jackson's Hermitage was made from the wood of this stately tree, and the name Tulip Grove, given to Andrew Jackson Donelson's estate adjoining the Hermitage, was taken from a grove of tulip poplars on the property. The name was suggested by President Martin Van Buren during a visit with Jackson.

Despite its name, the tulip poplar is a member of the magnolia family. Its scientific name is *Liriodendron tulipifera*, from the Greek words for "lily tree" and "bearing tulips." It's most easily identified by its odd-shaped leaves, which look like the ends have been cut off. They sometimes dance on their slender stalks like poplar leaves, which is where part of the confusion arose. After the leaves reach their full four- to six-inch width in late May or early June, the tree's tuliplike flowers appear. There are three sepals and six greenish-yellow petals with orange spots at the base. In the center of each flower are pistils that will develop into a cone-shaped cluster of dry fruits about three inches long. The leaves turn bright orange-yellow in the fall, and in the winter, there are flattened buds at the tips of the twigs that resemble little green spatulas.

The biggest tulip poplar in the state is one of the biggest in the country: it is 135 feet tall with a 71-foot branch spread, and its circumference at 4½ feet above the ground is 25 feet three inches. It's located in Cocke County, near the H. Albright Grove Nature Trail in the Great Smoky Mountains National Park.

That tree, however, would have been dwarfed by some of the giants existing when the first European settlers arrived. The virgin forest was filled with trees of impressive stature, and tulip poplars grew to nearly 200 feet. As part of the Tennessee Centennial Exhibition in 1897, the Nashville, Chattanooga and St. Louis Railroad exhibited a tulip poplar log 10 feet four inches in diameter—nearly 33 feet in circumference. It had been taken from a stand in Crockett County.

During that same year, the American Forestry Association, meeting in Nashville, was told that "huge tulip-trees, with ages numbered in centuries, crowd the deep coves and rich mountainsides with their gigantic forms," but the end was already in sight. The wide-ranging usefulness of tulip poplars and the coming of the railroads after the Civil War marked the end of the virgin forests. When logging got underway in earnest in the 1880s, just the big, old trees were taken. Those less than 30 inches in diameter were left standing. By

1905, though, the situation had changed so much that mills were happy to get 14-inch trees. Much of Tennessee was clear-cut, and the only virgin forests remaining are in a few remote parts of the Smokies and in places like deep gulfs in portions of the Fall Creek Falls area.

Fortunately for tourists, naturalists and loggers alike, the tulip poplar is a hardy, quick-growing tree. The light, winged seeds will float into most any clear, well-watered site and take over. They can grow 3-4 feet a year, and a poplar stand a few decades old will yield many times the wood of a much older oak-hickory stand. That makes for a thriving poplar business. There are, for instance, half a dozen mills within 10 miles of each other near Clarksville cutting yellow poplar, as the tree is known to lumbermen because of its yellow heartwood. Although they'll take 12-inch diameter trees for mill work and even smaller for pulp, there are still stands with trees 3-4 feet in diameter near Fort Campbell, and trees with 20- to 30-inch diameters are not at all uncommon.

Those mills have ready markets for yellow poplar, which is lightweight (26-28 pounds per cubic foot), softer even than most softwoods, and easily worked. It's used for furniture, cabinets, flooring and trim, turnery, doors, siding, shingles and vehicle bodies, among other things, and it has recently been approved for house framing, although it has not yet caught on in that capacity. During World War II, it was used extensively in the manufacture of airplanes. Lower-grade wood is used as core stock for plywood, slack cooperage staves, boxes, crates and excelsior, and the pulpwood is good for high-grade book paper.

The tulip poplar is scattered widely all over the state, with the exception of the Nashville Basin, where it's less common because the soil is a little too dry and rocky. Nashville, though, has long been associated with the tree because of the city's importance as a shipping center. In the late 19th century, Nashville had become the largest hardwood market in the world, and in 1897, 27 million board feet of lumber were shipped from the capital, with the tulip poplar accounting for more than half of that.

The drive to name a state tree didn't get under way until the mid-1940s, and there was the usual political maneuvering involved. "A split between the white oak faction and the black walnut faction . . . blocked all legislative action during the two preceding sessions," according to a 1947 article in the *Nashville Tennessean*. The cedar and hickory were suggested as compromises, but the tulip poplar's intimate association with so many early and famous Tennesseans, and its commercial importance, led to its ultimate victory in 1947.

Bicentennial Tree: Yellowwood

In 1991, the Legislature designated the yellowwood tree as the state's official bicentennial tree, calling it "a native Tennessee ornamental tree of unsurpassed beauty, worthy of being grown in yards and public spaces across Tennessee." In selecting it, they expressed the wish that it serve "as a tribute to the pioneering spirit of those individuals whose courage and perseverance paved the way for the settlement of the great state of Tennessee."

The yellowwood, *Cladrastis lutea*, is a medium-sized tree, reaching a maximum height of 55-60 feet and a maximum diameter of three feet. It prefers moist soils, and is often found along stream banks, in rich rocky coves or in deep mountain valleys like those in many parts of the Great Smoky Mountains. It grows from southwestern Virginia to Oklahoma, from southern Indiana to northeast Georgia. It is a member of the legume family, a large group including redbuds and locusts as well as crops like clover, alfalfa, peas and beans. It has compound leaves nearly a foot in length with 7-11 smooth-edged leaflets, each 2-4 inches long and 1-2 inches wide. The fragrant, white, five-petaled flowers are in branched clusters about a foot long, and the tree produces 3-inch flattened pods that hang in clusters and contain 4-6 bean-like seeds.

The tree's bark is gray, thin and smooth, resembling that of beech. Its heartwood, as its name implies, is yellow, and it turns light brown on exposure. It is used as a source of dye. Its prime use, though, is as one of the loveliest ornamentals in parks and yards around the state.

Wild Animal: Raccoon

Few wild creatures have endeared themselves to human beings the way raccoons have. They are familiar nocturnal visitors to many campsites and rural homes, their pelts come into fashion as clothing every so often, their quick wits make them sought-after game animals, and their food-washing habits and black bandit's masks give them a deceptively charming appearance.

It's small wonder that when the Tennessee Legislature

decided in 1971 to designate a state wild animal, it chose the raccoon.

Through the years, more people have tried to domesticate the raccoon than all but a handful of other wild animals. While it's illegal to take raccoons from the wild to domesticate them in Tennessee, it's legal to purchase them from the many out-of-state suppliers in existence. A short discussion with someone who's done that, though, would probably convince most people not to, for it's in attempting to domesticate them that people find out a raccoon's charm is only skin-deep.

A raccoon is as curious and innovative an animal as there is, and one can turn a house inside out in no time, opening doors, drawers and cupboards, knocking things over and pulling down curtains. And after awhile, a bored raccoon may start biting its hosts, wearing out whatever welcome it has left.

The home front aside, the raccoon has played an important part in this continent's fashion and commercial arenas since before the arrival of the first European settlers. Powhatan is said to have presented Captain John Smith with a coonskin robe in the early 1600s, and by the time of the American Revolution, the coonskin cap—with the tail hanging rakishly to one side—was quite common. During the settling of many of the Mississippi Valley states, coonskins were used for currency, and one of Tennessee's homegrown legends, frontiersman/politician Davy Crockett, is known as much for his affinity for coonskin as anything.

The increasing urbanization and sophistication of the 20th century have not meant the loss of coonskin as a fashion item. The raccoon coats that were all the rage among college-aged males in the 1920s drove the price of pelts through the roof and placed heavy hunting pressure on the raccoon population. When they went out of style, raccoon fur lost much of its value, except during a short spurt in the '50s when Davy Crockett caps came into vogue again.

These days the raccoon hunting that goes on is either for

food or for sport. Raccoons, which resemble bears in many behavioral activities, are crafty enough to provide a good long chase for hunting dogs, giving some hunters, not so incidentally, the chance to sit around a fire and swap tall tales while waiting for the dogs to get one treed. The meat, said to taste like a combination of chicken and lamb, is highly prized by many hunters.

Terry Livingstone

Pound for pound, a raccoon can whip a hunting dog, particularly if he can get it in water, where he'll sometimes climb on its head and drown it. The dogs' size and numbers, though, usually turn the tide.

The hunting and trapping seasons vary in East, Middle and West Tennessee, but are generally from late October or early November through mid-January or mid-February. Limits per person or per party vary as well, with East Tennessee, where the raccoon's numbers aren't as great, having more restrictive regulations. When it's not being hunted, the raccoon's predators include the great horned owl, the fox and the bobcat.

Raccoons are common from southern Canada to Central America, except for a few pockets of the Rockies. Most have their nesting sites in tree cavities, but many use ground dens, and they can be found in caves, mines and woodchuck burrows, and in and under barns or other buildings, provided there's water nearby. They are not true hibernators but will retreat to the den for a time during snowy, sub-freezing periods. They sleep during the day, curled in a ball, or on their backs with their forepaws over their eyes, and feed at night. They are omnivorous, consuming fish, frogs and crawfish, fruit, nuts and berries, insects, and even birds and small mammals. They are especially fond of corn and will stuff themselves with sweet or field corn, given the opportunity.

The raccoon handles its food quite extensively before eating it, and since this is often done in or near water, the notion that it "washes" its food before eating took hold. In fact, the word *lotor*, in its Latin name, *Procyon lotor*, means "washer." The dexterous use of its forepaws also gave way to the Algonquin Indian name for the raccoon, *arakunem*, which means "he who scratches with his hands."

An adult raccoon in Tennessee will get to be from 26 to 38 inches long, including a 10-inch tail, and weigh 12 pounds or so. Large males may reach 16 or 18 pounds.

Males normally adopt home ranges of from 1.5 to 2 square miles, although they may wander more widely during the breeding season, which lasts from late January until March.

The raccoon's gestation period is 64 days, and most litters consist of 3-4 young (although 2-6 are possible). The young are born with fuzzy fur and well-defined masks, and can crawl around and do a little tree-climbing even before their eyes open at about 19 days.

A safe, content young raccoon will make a churring sound, as will the adults, which can also growl, hiss, and make a noise reminiscent of the screech owl.

By the time it's six weeks old, a young raccoon is able and

willing to get into all kinds of scrapes. A favorite pastime is climbing well up a tree it can't climb back down, then squealing for mama, who comes and takes the wayward young'un in tow by the scruff of the neck. At the approach of danger, the mother will hurry the young up the nearest tree for safety.

It's the kind of behavior that would make any animal endearing, particularly one that sports a mask and a ringed tail. It's also one of the reasons why the raccoon is one of Tennessee's most popular state symbols.

The convergent ladybird beetle, one of many species of ladybug.

Insect: Ladybug

Ladybugs have been called the most beneficial of all beetles, and it's not hard to figure out why. Since the dawn of agriculture, their voracious appetites for crop pests have made them invaluable to our food-growing efforts, and they're being used more and more today as biologically sound alternatives to pesticides.

Their usefulness in Tennessee agriculture led the state Legislature to designate the ladybug, or ladybird beetle, as state insect in 1975 (it shares that distinction with the firefly).

These small, oval insects with the bright, spotted shells have long been welcome guests in agricultural settings. Their name is a reflection of the religious bent that gratitude for their services took, for in Europe they were dedicated to the Virgin Mary as "Our Lady's Beetles."

The familiar children's rhyme, "Ladybug, ladybug, fly away home / Your house is on fire, your children will burn" also grew out of the European farming experience. After crop harvesting, it was customary to burn what was left to clear the field and destroy any insect pests. Ladybug larvae, which are unable to fly, were also burnt.

There are 475 species of ladybugs, or *Coccinellidae*, in the continental U.S., and all but two are beneficial. None, though, provides a more dramatic example of usefulness than *Rodolia cardinalis*, which saved California's citrus crop 100 years ago.

The cottony-cushion scale, introduced accidentally from Australia in 1868, was wiping out peach, lime, orange and other trees. By the mid-1880s, farmers had tried every compound they had, but the pest was still so bad that many just gave up. An American biologist in Australia saw that *Rodolia cardinalis* fed on the scale, and a few hundred were shipped to California. Within two years, the pest was under complete control, and the citrus industry was saved.

In Tennessee, proof of the ladybug's worth has been less dramatic, but scientists are at work now looking for similar predatory relationships. Dr. Paris Lambden of the University of Tennessee is overseeing a project that has imported a species from Korea that is effective against the willow scale, a pest to euonymous, a decorative shrub.

Indigenous species of ladybugs are, of course, useful in controlling many pests as well. In Tennessee, *Adalia bipunctata*, a two-spotted orange, black and white beetle, feeds on aphids, including the green peach aphid. The convergent ladybug, with two narrow white lines on its neck, feeds on aphids

Russell Bromby

that harm tobacco crops. The spotted ladybug, pink with white spots, feeds on corn leaf aphids. There are dozens of other crops, trees and shrubs that benefit from the ladybug's appetite for predators.

Much of the research involving ladybugs is designed to "target" their use. By studying their eating preferences, scientists can release them where needed. The use of predatory species from overseas is necessary because fully a third of the crop pests in the U.S. were imported, usually accidentally. Often they have no natural predators in their new surroundings, and their old ones must be found and brought in.

Their usefulness has made ladybugs a hot commercial item in some parts of the country, particularly in the West. Many are sold to farmers or individuals by the thousand for specific pest control purposes. The problem with this, according to Lambden and co-researcher Dr. Jamie Yanes, formerly of the Ellington Agricultural Center in Nashville, is that the ladybugs will eat the pest, then fly away, laying their eggs elsewhere and leaving the next generation of pests without a predator. "They benefit somebody," Yanes says, "but rarely the person who paid for them."

Ladybugs work best en masse, and the sight of thousands gathered on a Tennessee apple tree in the spring is a dramatic one. They're drawn together by sex pheromones. A female will release the pheromone, and males can detect it from several miles away. Other females release more, and soon they're bunched in huge numbers.

After mating, the female lays eggs on the underside of a leaf or in a bark crevice. Since the young don't have wings, the eggs are always laid on a pest-infested plant or tree so that food is close at hand. The young are insatiable, devouring eggs, aphids, mites and scale insects. Each female lays hundreds of eggs, and each of the larvae may eat thousands of pests. After a few weeks, each reaches full size, then hangs itself up by the tail to the surface of a leaf and transforms into a short, stout chrysalis. This pupal stage lasts 10-14 days, when the shell that develops splits and the winged, adult ladybug emerges.

The adults that make it through the summer will hibernate during the winter, and a valuable peculiarity ensures that many will make it: ladybugs secrete a foul-tasting substance that makes them unpalatable to birds. Some species hibernate in large clusters, but many hide singly under bark, in old haystacks, or in houses or other buildings. A ladybug hibernating in a pioneer house was thought of as a sign of good luck.

In Tennessee, the use of ladybugs and other "alternative methodologies" is barely getting started. The state's farmers still rely almost exclusively on chemical pesticides. Lambden says, however, that Tennessee growers "are becoming more and more aware of the need to utilize environmentally sound control policies. More people are concerned about what they're putting on their orchards and field crops."

As this concern turns into action, more and more

Tennessee farmers will be turning to a source of pest predation that's as old as farming itself—Tennessee's smallest state symbol, the ladybug.

Insect: Firefly

There are a few sights and smells and tastes that stand out. They startle us awake when our senses have taken to sleepwalking. They are the things that say to us, "Life is worth living."

Rich, red sunsets are like that, and blueberry pies, and velvet. Fireflies are in that category, especially for those of us fortunate enough to live where they are abundant. No matter how many times you see them, fireflies are a thrill. They're hard to take for granted. There are few moments to match the one in early summer when we first see them, rising like champagne bubbles, imparting to the darkness the warm aura of a fairy tale kingdom. Crickets and cicadas are transformed into a symphony backing up their delicately elegant light show.

Children in this country catch them in jars. Women in the West Indies sometimes pin them to their dresses or their hair to wear them as living jewelry to balls. Parents in some parts of Japan catch great numbers of them and turn them loose inside the mosquito netting around their children's beds, so that they're escorted to dreamland by the cool lanterns of these magic creatures.

It's a pretty glamorous life for an insect that spends its days hiding sluggishly under leaves.

The firefly isn't a fly at all; it's a member of the order *Coleoptera*—the beetles. And while it's just one of the more than 300,000 members of that order, its specialty is so captivating that it gets more good press than just about any of the others. It was named state insect, along with the ladybug, which is also a beetle, in 1975.

There are more than 1,500 species in the lightning bug family, *Lampyridae*, with 136 in North America and most of those in the eastern United States. Its light is a scientific marvel in that it is "cool"—it doesn't give off heat the way most lights do. The incandescent light bulb in your home, for instance, wastes about 90 percent of its energy in the form of heat, with only about 10 percent turned into light. The firefly's light is almost totally efficient, producing little or no heat. That's the result of the interplay of three compounds: in the presence of luciferase, luciferin combines with oxygen to form a compound that gives off light as it decomposes; ATP (adenosine triphosphate), an energy storage compound present in every living cell, makes luciferin available for use.

That chemical interplay has also given the lightning bug a role in the U.S. space program. The luciferase and a precursor of luciferin are extracted from fireflies and purified, providing the most sensitive material yet discovered for testing for ATP. When the Mariner probe searched for life on Mars, it did so with compounds taken from fireflies.

Extracts from fireflies are also used in the study of heart disease, muscular dystrophy and urinary infections. They also help test the effectiveness of antibiotics and waste-water treatment methods, and aid in the early diagnosis of hypothermia in swine, which costs the pork industry $300 million a year.

The fireflies you see blinking in the night air are males. Females perch on or near the ground; many, in fact, are wingless. The male rises as it flashes, trying to interest a female in flashing back. Each species has its own code. For instance, the male of *Photinus pyralis* flashes every six seconds, and an interested female will respond two seconds later.

Once mating has taken place, the male begins looking for another receptive female. Some females engage in a far more deadly activity known as "aggressive mimicry." After mating, a female will sometimes answer the flashing code of a different species, and when a love-hungry male lands, he's eaten. One of the reasons this is a worthwhile endeavor is that there can be as many as 50 males to every female on a given summer night. That's not so good for the males, but it's great for the females and for human firefly watchers.

Eggs are laid on or just under damp soil and hatch in about three weeks; the larvae are already able to glow. Since an adult firefly uses its flashing beacon as a sexual attractant, scientists aren't sure why larvae can also emit light. One theory is that the glow tells predators that this potential meal doesn't taste good.

The larvae live among rotting vegetation, feeding on snails, slugs, worms, aphids and larval insects until fall, when they burrow into the ground for the winter. After two such hibernations, they emerge and prepare for the pupal stage. They again go underground, this time into small earthen cells, and emerge 10-20 days later as adults.

And that emergence sets aglow another summer of magic.

Agricultural Insect: Honeybee

It would be hard to overstate the importance of honeybees. Even in a world of artificial sweeteners and synthetic waxes, honey and beeswax remain valued commodities, the former for its natural, nutritional sweetness, and the latter for its purity in applications from candles to lithography.

Still, there's something far more vital to humans that occurs in the daily comings and goings of these little dynamos. In the course of producing honey and wax, honeybees perform their really important service—they pollinate the plants that produce much of what we eat and some of what we wear.

Recognizing that vital role, the Tennessee Legislature named the honeybee the state agricultural insect in 1990. They were prompted by Dickson County Area Beekeepers president Kenneth Greene, who stalked the halls of the Legislature with an embroidered skep (the old-style beehive of twisted straw) on the back of his bee pin-studded vest, passing out honey candy and making his case to any legislator who'd listen. The bill passed the House 92-0, and Greene was named Beekeeper of the Year by the Tennessee State Beekeepers Association for his efforts.

Honey was mankind's first sweetener, a gift of nature so hard-won that it was among the most precious substances in many cultures. It symbolized goodness and plenty, as in the land "flowing with milk and honey" that the Hebrews were promised in Exodus, and was used in making fermented mead, a highly prized drink in cultures from Rome to Scandinavia. It adds a wholesome sweetness in baking and cooking, and has been a part of many health and beauty aids, from cough syrups to skin lotions. It was even employed as an embalming fluid in ancient Egypt, and could be used for paying taxes in some cultures.

Beeswax, too, has had its role in taxation. A shortage of money in Tennessee in 1785 led the Legislature of the then-territory to permit taxes to be paid in beeswax. Long before that secular use, though, it was an integral part of some religious ceremonies, as its use was specified in the candles used in some churches. It has also been part of the make-up of a variety of products including artificial fruits and flowers, modelling wax, leather dressings, waxed paper, furniture and floor waxes, lithographic inks, cosmetics, ointments, paints, polishes and both adhesives and lubricants.

Oddly enough, the honeybee is not native to America. The common "domestic" honeybee—*Apis mellifera* (from the

Latin words for bee and honey-bearer)—was brought to America by early European colonists. The original strain was Italian, but many hybrids have been developed since. Native Americans, who were unfamiliar with honeybees, called them "the white man's fly."

Approximately one-half inch long, the honeybee, like all insects, has three sections—head, thorax, and abdomen—and six legs. It has keen eyesight, with two large compound eyes and three simple eyes on top of the head, and it has two sensitive, odor-detecting antennae.

In the wild, bees are found in hives they build into hollowed trees and logs. As mankind domesticated the bee, skeps came into common use, and the modern hive is a wooden-frame unit with removable sections. In any hive, worker bees, consuming honey, secrete beeswax in tiny flakes from the underside of the abdomen and mold it into a honeycomb, which consists of thin-walled, back-to-back, six-sided cells. Propolis, a plant resin found in the buds of trees and collected by the workers, is also used in construction. Some cells are used for storing honey and pollen, and the queen lays eggs, normally one per cell, in the others. The protein-rich pollen, found in the anthers of flowers, is necessary for the rearing of young bees, and is generally stored around the broodnest, low in the hive, where the eggs develop. The honey is stored toward the top of the hive.

Worker bees, all female, travel from plant to plant gathering nectar, a sugary solution found in nectaries in the blossoms and sometimes on the leaves or stems. During its six-week life, each bee gathers enough for about a 12th of a teaspoon of honey, and a hive travels a total of about 55,000 air miles to collect each pound. A large colony may contain 60,000 workers, which can collect 1,000 pounds of nectar, pollen and water (which is used in cooling the hive) during the course of a summer. When a worker returns to the hive, the nectar it has gathered is transferred to a "house bee," which transfers it to a cell. It's thought that both the field and

Terry Livingstone

house bees add enzymes which help in turning the nectar to
honey, a process involving the inversion of the bulk of the
nectar's sucrose into fructose and glucose. Another vital ele-
ment in the transformation is the reduction of the moisture
content. Nectar is about 80 percent water, while finished
honey contains between 16 and 18 percent. The process used
is simple evaporation: Using their wings inside the hive,
house bees create drafts that evaporate moisture, and when

the percentage of water is right, the cells are capped.

Honeybees, which transmit information about plant location and distance (they may travel several miles) with little "dances," generally stay with one species at a time, a very valuable habit in pollination and in ensuring a consistency in honey production. Most "supermarket" honey is clover, which makes for a sweet, mild, light-colored honey. Generally, darker, amber-colored honeys like buckwheat contain greater amounts of minerals and have a stronger and more distinct taste. Among the lightest of the honeys is that made from cotton.

Some $2 million in honey is gathered in Tennessee each year by the state's beekeepers. The dramatically higher value of honeybees as crop pollinators can be seen in the fact that crops relying on them for pollination are worth about $100 million per year in the state.

Pollination occurs because in traveling from blossom to blossom, honeybees come in contact with dustlike particles of pollen, which stick to bristly hairs on their heads, thoraxes and legs. Some of these will brush off at the next plant, while new ones are picked up, ensuring the cross-pollination vital to many plant species.

Of the roughly one million colonies used for pollination nationwide, a large percentage are used for alfalfa and in fruit and nut trees, with almonds and apples leading the way. There are, however, 90 U.S. crops dependent upon insect pollination, and honeybees are by far the most important and dependable pollinators. They are also valuable in pollinating some forest and range plants that provide food for wildlife.

Beekeepers are often contracted by farmers and growers to place hives within or adjacent to crop fields to be pollinated. One hive of bees can pollinate an acre of apple trees, while two or more may be necessary for many other crops.

There are three kinds of bees in a hive. Workers, by far the most populous segment of the population, are sexually undeveloped females. They are produced when eggs laid by the queen are fertilized with drones' sperm. Drones, stingless males which are slightly larger than females, are produced from the unfertilized eggs of the queen and, in some cases, of egg-laying workers. Their only function is to mate with the queen, and they die in the process.

Eggs, which the queen can produce at the rate of 1,000 per day, hatch into larvae in three days. All are fed royal jelly, which is produced in the salivary glands of workers, mixed with pollen and honey. When fully grown, the larvae enter the pupal stage. Queens emerge by chewing their way out of the cell after 16 days, workers after 21, and drones after 23-24.

Workers spend their first three weeks or so as "house bees," feeding and cleaning the queen, feeding pupa and larvae, making wax, transferring nectar from field bees to cells, cleaning and repairing the hive, carrying out dead bees, guarding the entrance, and fanning their wings to keep an airflow within the hive.

When multiple queens emerge, they fight until there is only one remaining in the hive. The new queen attacks the old, which leaves with a swarm to form a new colony. When cold weather comes, all the workers surround the queen and whatever eggs are left in a slowly moving ball, maintaining her at a temperature of 86-90 degrees. Bees born late in the year live longer than the normal six weeks, lasting through the winter until new eggs laid by the queen begin hatching.

Modern beekeeping methods involve artificial insemination of queens, the replacement of queens every year or two (they live up to five ordinarily), their breeding and mail-order selling, and the selling of bees by the pound for restocking. Safe handling methods involve veils, gloves and, depending on the temperament of the bees and the preference of the keeper, smokers.

The worker bee has a barbed stinger used in defending herself and the hive. When she stings, the stinger is torn from her, killing her, and muscles attached to the stinger continue to drive it into the skin for several minutes as the venom sac pumps venom, so the stinger should be scraped from the skin at once in the event of a sting. Many people who work around bees develop immunity to the stings, but normally there is pain, reddening of the skin, and some swelling. People who are allergic to honeybees may develop skin splotches, breathing difficulties, irregular heartbeat and shock.

Bees have a number of natural enemies, including ants, wax moths, dragonflies, mantises and certain wasps and yellow jackets. Among mammals, mice will sometimes enter hives in winter, skunks will eat large numbers of bees at the hive entrance, and bears will decimate hives, eating bees and honey.

It is mites and, to a lesser extent, fungi and bacteria, though, that pose the real problem to beekeepers in Tennessee. Tracheal mites, which lay eggs in bees' tracheal tubes, causing them to suffocate when they hatch, first appeared in the state in December 1987, and by the early '90s they were wreaking havoc with the state's beekeepers. Greene's own hives were wiped out, membership in the Dickson beekeepers' group was cut in half, and beekeepers statewide found their hives seriously affected.

Treatment measures undertaken by beekeepers have brought back the bees somewhat—Greene was back to five hives by mid-1994 and was planning to extract honey for the first time in two years—but there are ongoing concerns about the health of the state's honeybees.

Those problems, along with the continued movement northward of Africanized bees (killer bees), which could interbreed with domestic bees and which may or may not be able to survive Tennessee winters, mean that a great deal of care will have to be taken to insure the well-being, over the next several years, of the state symbol that means so much to Tennessee's agricultural economy—the honeybee.

Butterfly: Zebra Swallowtail

The process of selecting a state butterfly was much more than a beauty contest. Students in Mrs. Sherrill Charlton's biology class at Gallatin High School, who were faced with the responsibility, sought opinions from other schools in Sumner County, then narrowed their list to three candidates and began weighing the evidence.

The gulf fritillary, a red-orange butterfly with black dots above and brilliant white streaks and ovals below, had a tie-in with another state symbol working in its favor, since it feeds on the passionflower, the state wildflower. The monarch, that orange and black butterfly with the stained-glass look, had familiarity and beauty on its side. The zebra swallowtail, a black-and-white butterfly with splashes of red and blue, had the swordlike tail and an appearance every bit as striking as the other two.

The turning point came with study of each butterfly's range and habits. The monarch is a migrant with a very wide distribution. The gulf fritillary is at home into Mexico and parts of the far West. The zebra swallowtail, while having a wide distribution throughout the eastern and central parts of the country, is particularly abundant in the South, and it lays its eggs on the pawpaw and its relatives.

"You can't get much more Southern than the pawpaw," said Mrs. Charlton, and, with that bit of evidence, the students—and the state—had their butterfly.

In choosing the zebra swallowtail (*Eurytides marcellus*), the class completed a process that got underway when Mrs. Charlton, visiting the butterfly center at Calloway Gardens near Atlanta in 1993, decided Tennessee should join the ranks of states which have butterflies among their state symbols. [See Chapter 19—How We Get Symbols—for the complete story of its selection.] They also gave the state an especially beautiful symbol. The swallowtails are our largest and most attractive butterflies, and the zebra is one of the most striking of the group. Alternate black and white stripes run the length of its body, and there are pairs of red and blue dots on its lower back. Underneath, there is an additional red stripe running up the middle of the rear wings. The tail, black with a white border, can be an inch long, about a third of the zebra's length.

Like all butterflies, the zebra swallowtail is an insect, a member of the large phylum *Arthropoda*, which also includes spiders and crustaceans. The adult has three body segments—head, thorax and abdomen—and six legs. Two antennae, extending from the head, are apparently used in smelling and for tactile orientation. Two large compound eyes feature thousands of facets, each of which acts as a tiny lens, giving butterflies, it is thought, one color image which includes the ultraviolet spectrum. Extending from beneath each eye is a furry palpus that helps protect the proboscis, which is tongue-like and works like a drinking straw when the butterfly uncoils it to drink nectar and other liquids.

The thorax contains the legs and four wings. Each leg is jointed and ends in a tarsus, which has claws and is sensitive to taste. Wings are comprised of membranes, and the bright colors help the sexes identify each other and serve in camouflage and mimicry. Millions of tiny scales overlap like shingles on each wing, and among those are sex scales, which produce pheromones, scent hormones that generate mate-attracting scents.

The abdomen, consisting of 11 segments, takes in air through spiracles along its sides and contains both digestive and sexual organs.

The zebra is a relatively abundant swallowtail, with a range that extends from southern Canada in the Great Lakes region to the Gulf Coast, and from the East Coast to the eastern Great Plains. It can generally be seen from April through October in the northern part of its range, and from March through December along the Gulf Coast. It is a denizen of meadows and marshes, riverbanks and lakeshores.

The zebra swallowtail larva, or caterpillar, grows from a tiny green egg laid on the leaf of a pawpaw or related species. It is striped and has simple eyes, chewing jaws, three pairs of jointed legs in the front and five pairs of grasping "prolegs" in the back. It also has a small organ behind the head which emits a musky odor some predators find offensive. The caterpillar is a feeding machine which, because its skin is inelastic, grows by molting, or shedding its skin, several times until it is about two inches long. With the final molt, the caterpillar enters the pupal stage, becoming a green-to-brown, inch-long chrysalis. Over the course of the following winter, the chrysalis is transformed inside its protective cocoon into an adult butterfly. Courtship begins soon afterward, and the entire process repeats itself.

Butterflies have many natural enemies, including birds, spiders, other insects and toads, but it is man that has the biggest impact—the zebra swallowtail does not do well in the face of suburban sprawl and development. Still, in many of Tennessee's rural areas, this lovely butterfly is a vibrant, colorful symbol of the state's natural riches.

Dave Murrian, Tennessee Wildlife Resources Agency

Game Bird: Bobwhite Quail

T he bobwhite quail, named Tennessee's state game bird by the 95th General Assembly in 1987, has had a rough time of it in recent years. Small-game populations in general have been hard-hit as the consolidation of farm fields and the use of agricultural chemicals have eliminated many of the weedy pockets and wide fencerows that normally provide food and cover for them. The Federal Farm Acts of 1985 and 1990, which encourage conservation practices that are beneficial to quail, have helped somewhat, but it's estimated that suburban sprawl has taken perhaps 20 percent of suitable quail habitat since 1970. Still, the designation of the bobwhite as a state symbol by the Legislature acknowledges the importance of this bird to hunters and other outdoor enthusiasts.

The bobwhite was one of a number of birds considered in the 1930s for selection as state bird, an honor ultimately won by the mockingbird in statewide balloting. The bobwhite's obvious selling points were its status as a highly prized game bird and the well-known whistled "bob-WHITE!" call that gives it its common name. Its scientific name, *Colinus virginianus*, is the Latinized version of the Spanish and French *colin*, or quail, and of the state of Virginia, where it was particularly plentiful.

The bobwhite lives throughout the East and in parts of the West in a variety of weeded areas, from pastures and meadows to prairie grasslands. Its fall and winter diet consists primarily of wild and domestic grass and tree seeds, legumes and wild fruits and berries. At this time, it can sometimes be attracted to backyard feeders with seeds and grains. In the spring, quail will also feed on clovers and succulent grasses; insects such as grasshoppers, ants and spiders also make up a significant part of the diet of nesting hens and chicks.

A rather stocky, reddish-brown bird with short legs and rounded wings, the bobwhite is about 10 inches long, with a 14-inch wingspan. It weighs from six to seven ounces. The male has a white stripe over its eyes and a white patch on its throat, while those features are buff-colored in the female. Otherwise, the sexes look alike. The birds generally live just one or two summers in the wild, although individuals have survived for eight or more years in captivity.

The male opens the spring with its "bob-WHITE! bob-WHITE!" call, issued as a territorial challenge to other males. In April or May, the birds, which had been assembled into winter coveys, break up into pairs. State figures compiled in the 1970s (habitat data on which to base current estimates are now being assembled, and are expected to reflect the 20 percent drop mentioned above) estimated 900,000 pairs of quail in Tennessee in the spring.

The male's courtship display involves spreading its wings and turning them forward, with the tips touching the ground, spreading the tail, turning the head to display the white markings, and making short rushes toward the female. Males may fight fiercely during the springtime as they defend their territories against other males.

The nest is built in a shallow depression in the ground dug by either of the pair in a well-concealed place. It is normally about six inches in diameter and two inches high, built and lined with dried grasses, straw, leaves and weed stalks, and concealed with weeds and grasses woven into an arch over it. A small opening is left on the side.

Tennessee Wildlife Resources Agency

If the nest should be destroyed for some reason, the pair will build it a second, third, or even fourth time.

The bobwhite is one of the most prodigious egg-layers in the bird world. Starting five days after nest construction begins, the female lays from 10 to 20 cream-colored, inch-long eggs, one a day. It's estimated that some nine million eggs are laid in Tennessee yearly, although 60 percent will never hatch because of predators including dogs and cats, human-related nest disturbances, and extremes of weather. Still, the quail population more than triples by August.

Somewhere between one and seven days after the last egg

is laid, the female begins incubation, which takes 23 days and is often assisted by the male. All the eggs hatch on the same day, and the chicks are able to come out of the nest with their parents a few hours after being hatched. Adults use the "crippled bird" ploy to try to lure predators from the nest and young birds. Chicks can fly at two weeks of age, and they begin to feed as a covey at three weeks. They weigh as much as adults and fully resemble them at 12 to 15 weeks of age.

By September, when the breeding season is over, individuals from family coveys mix with individuals from others and form coveys of up to 25-30 birds for the fall and winter. Groups of 10-20 birds assemble in cover just before nightfall to roost, heads out, in tight circles. If disturbed, the covey may scurry into thicker cover and freeze momentarily, then explode loudly in all directions, to regroup the next morning.

About an hour after sunrise, coveys (the same holds true for pairs earlier in the season) travel on foot to a favorite feeding spot and eat for an hour or two, find a resting spot at midday, then return about two hours before sunset for another meal. Like other non-migratory game birds, bobwhite are strong fliers for short distances only (they have been timed at top speeds of 30 to 50 miles per hour); walking in cover exposes them to less predation.

The death rate for quail remains high through the nesting period, then tapers off in October as juveniles become able to take care of themselves and adults are freed of chick-rearing responsibilities. Food and cover are generally abundant at this time of year, and the weather is usually warm and dry. Rougher weather and the thinning of food and cover bring the number down further by the end of November. If food is particularly scarce, bobwhite may travel on foot to a new food source, but the species is not migratory.

Quail hunting season in Tennessee runs (at the time of this printing) from the second Saturday in November through the end of February, and approximately one-third to one-half of the state's November population is harvested—about the same number that would die if there were no hunting season, according to state figures.

Those that survive the harsh winter weather, reduction of food, diseases, accidents and the state's hunters are those nature has determined are best-suited to start the reproductive cycle again in the spring. And while those factors all take their toll on the bobwhite population in the normal yearly life cycle, one factor—adequate, available habitat—will make the difference in the population of this Tennessee state symbol through the coming years.

Channel catfish

Fish: Channel Catfish and Largemouth Bass

Late in 1987, avid fishermen Ricky Chadwick and Jason Mobley were looking through the *Tennessee Blue Book* when they discovered that, for all its symbols, Tennessee didn't have a state fish. Their discussion was overheard by Mrs. Elaine Baggett, librarian at the Erin Elementary School library, where the seventh-graders were at the time.

"I told them there were a couple of second-graders that had campaigned for the ladybug [one of two state insects], and I said, 'Why don't you see what you can do?' " They wrote letters to Senator Riley Darnell of Clarksville and Representative Bill Collier of Waverly during the second week of December, and by the time they got back to school from Christmas break, the three learned that a bill was in the works.

By March of 1988, the state had two new symbols—the channel catfish as commercial fish, and the largemouth bass as game fish.

Channel catfish, *Ictalurus punctatus*, are the best-looking members of an ugly family. The sleekest and most agile of the group, they are slate blue to gray on the back, with sides that vary from light blue to silver, and creamy white bellies. Their tails are deeply forked, and they have four pairs of whisker-like barbels, or feelers, which are used to detect and identify food. Like other catfish, channel cats have leathery, scale-less skin, and spines on their pectoral and dorsal fins that can inflict painful wounds, as anyone who's less-than-careful in handling them can attest.

Their common name comes from the fact that they tend to gravitate to the swiftest water in river channels, although they inhabit most Tennessee waters, from streams to our deepest TVA lakes. They flourish in farm ponds and are widely stocked and raised there. It is that role in aquaculture, being raised for shipment to restaurants and grocery stores, that gained them the nod as one of the state fish. In the sizes most familiar to restaurant-goers, they are often known as "fiddlers."

They don't feed as exclusively on the bottom as most of their relatives, and will eat insects, crawfish, mussels and live or dead fish, along with the usual bait delicacies like dough-balls, cheese, worms, grasshoppers and chicken livers. They also differ from their relatives in being a little more active during the day.

Vernon Summerlin

Franklin fishing guide Scott Morris with a Tennessee largemouth.

Channel cats spawn in late spring when the temperature in shallow water gets above 75 degrees, under overhanging rocks, in hollow logs, and in pockets under stumps or below rock structure. The males guard the young until they are able to fend for themselves.

Seasonal variations in water temperature regulate feeding as well. When the water drops below 55 degrees, catfish feed less, and when it hits 40 or so, they stop feeding altogether, with schools forming and remaining motionless in deep water.

Vernon Summerlin

The state record, by the way, is 41 pounds for a channel cat caught by Clint Walters, Jr. on July 30, 1982, at Fall Creek Falls Lake. The world record is 58 pounds for one taken from the Santee-Cooper Reservoir in South Carolina on July 7, 1964, by W. B. Whaley.

Largemouth bass, *Micropterus salmoides*, are probably the state's most sought-after game fish. Fast-growing, hard fighters that can adapt to many kinds of water, they are the center of attention at most fishing tournaments and in a number of outdoor magazines. Plastic worms and depth-finders have made them much more accessible to the average fisherman over the past few decades, and more and more people are experiencing the explosive strikes and heart-pounding leaps these fish are known for.

Large- and smallmouth bass are actually members of the sunfish family. The former are dark green to black above, with silver sides and belly and dark lateral bands that break up in older fish. The dorsal fin dips in the middle to the point where it is almost split. They inhabit streams, ponds, lakes and reservoirs statewide and will tolerate a variety of depths and clarity conditions. They prefer cover, and so are found along weedlines and dropoffs, among fallen trees and under boat docks. They often move to the shallows late at night and in the fall. In winter, when the water temperature falls below 50 degrees, they get very sluggish, schooling along dropoffs and points at least 15 feet deep when they're available. In summer, they will look for a depth where the water temperature holds at 68-75 degrees, making occasional feeding forays into warmer water.

Typical predators, they eat mostly smaller fishes, including those of their own species, some crustaceans, snails, salamanders and insects, although snakes, turtles, mice, and even birds have been found in their stomachs.

Largemouth reach 14-15 inches in length in three or four years, mature at two or three years of age, and have a maximum life span of 16 or 17 years. They spawn when the water temperature hits the mid-60s, with males excavating nests with their tails in sand or gravel near cover in shallow water. Healthy females can lay more than 30,000 eggs, moving into deeper water after doing so. The males release milt, then guard the nest vigorously; they have been known to die of exhaustion doing so.

The young stay on the nest until the yolk sacs are absorbed, then school in shallow water near cover, feeding on microscopic plankton, moving to small insects and fish when they reach two inches or so in length. Most bass live their entire lives within a few hundred yards of where they're hatched.

Largemouth have sensitive taste buds and excellent hearing, and can be spooked by loud noises. They're near-sighted, but can see a short distance out of the water, and are susceptible to being scared by bright lights at night.

The biggest largemouth ever taken in Tennessee was one weighing 14 pounds, eight ounces. Louge Barnett caught it on October 17, 1954, in Lawrence County's Sugar Creek.

The world record largemouth weighed an incredible 22 pounds, four ounces. It was taken from Montgomery Lake, Georgia, by George W. Perry, a 19-year-old farmer out in his homemade boat on June 2, 1932. He stopped at the general store on his way home and learned of a *Field & Stream* contest. Unmindful of the fees he could most likely have collected displaying it over the years, he mailed in a notarized certificate recording the fish's weight, girth and length, took it home and, with his family, ate it.

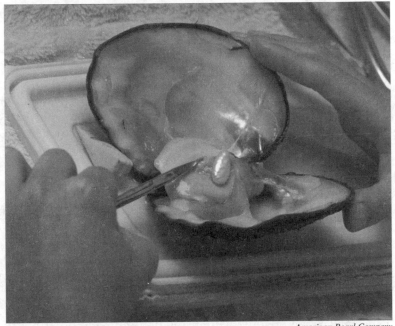

A freshwater pearl being harvested from a Tennessee mussel.

Gem: Freshwater Pearl

Charles Bradford and James Johnson were just looking for bait. The Murfreesboro boys were fishing in the Caney Fork River in the early 1880s when, on opening one of the mussels they had pulled from the mouth of Indian Creek, they found a large white pearl. They took it to William Wendel, a local druggist, who sent it off to Tiffany's in New York. A few days later the boys had a check for a then-impressive $83.

More than 100 years later, through boom and bust, and despite pollution, over-harvesting, TVA dams and the vicissitudes of fashion, mussels are bringing up to $40 million a year into Tennessee, and the freshwater pearl has been, since 1979, the official state gem. (Agate, a semiprecious gemstone, was named a state rock in 1969).

The kind of serendipity experienced by Charles and James had happened before in Tennessee, and it would happen again. A few years earlier, near Lancaster, a fisherman found a pearl that eventually sold for $2,000 in New York. Later, a farmer idly picking up a mussel while his horse drank was paid $190 for the pearl inside.

In each case, what followed was a rush to get in on the action, with many people from all walks of life spending their spare time in nearby rivers and creeks. They would dig the mollusks by hand or with forks or spades, split them with knives, and discard those that were pearl-less—the overwhelming majority of them.

Before long, the shallows had been stripped of mussels in many places, and people were using dredging and other methods to take them from deeper water. The process increased even more dramatically with the use of the mother-of-pearl from these shells in the manufacture of buttons.

Not long after the turn of the century, the rate of depletion was concerning a number of people. W. E. Myer of Carthage, speaking before the Tennessee Academy of Science in 1914, decried "the heedless total working out and total destruction of every mussel in each mussel bed and leaving no mussels to reproduce the race."

Despite his protestation, Myer, whose brother was a major New York pearl dealer, was one of many (explorer Hernando de Soto had been the first) to dig up the graves of Native American mound builders looking for the popular gem. Prehistoric residents had long been avid consumers of the mussels, both for food and for adornment, and archaeological excavations have often turned up large heaps of shells.

American Pearl Company

Sorting cultured blister pearls for quality.

Since pearls are a rare commodity, the selling of natural pearls would long be a minor sideline to the shell business, and once plastics replaced shell buttons on a large scale, it would take a new industry from the Far East to spark Tennessee's modern mussel business.

Pearls are formed when mollusks—clams, oysters, or mussels—secrete layer after layer of ultrathin nacre in an onionlike manner around an irritant, usually a tiny parasite or piece of shell. Waiting for nature to conduct that cycle is, of course, an exasperating business for those trying to make a living selling pearls, but it wasn't until the turn of the century that an effective process for "culturing," or manufacturing, pearls, was developed.

Two men working independently in Japan determined that secretions from the mantle—the tissue which lines the shell—create mother-of-pearl, from which the pearls themselves are made. Both men inserted tiny nuclei that mimicked the natural irritants and added a small piece of mantle particle from another mussel as well, successfully spurring pearl production. A third man, flamboyant entrepreneur Kokichi Mikimoto, received a Japanese patent for the first cultured round pearl in 1908 and took his case for the gem to the large American market, displaying creations like a pearl Statue of Liberty (nacre can be built up around a wide variety of shapes). As natural pearls became more scarce, cultured pearls took an ever-larger share of the market, dominating it almost completely by 1960.

The Japanese, who carefully guarded their production secrets, long dominated world markets. In the manufacturing process, though, they found themselves tied to Tennessee mussels. The Japanese make small pellets from shells and insert them as the starter irritants, and Tennessee's waters produce some of the best shells for the process, since they're less likely to be rejected and they produce more uniform pearls. In fact, some 40% of the shells used by the Japanese come from Tennessee companies.

There are over 70 species of mussels in Tennessee's waters, down from 127 a century ago. Nearly two dozen of those remaining are endangered or threatened, mostly because of pollution and TVA dams, which rob rivers of the swift water many of the mollusks rely on for feeding. There are a dozen species which can be removed from the riverbed, and four make up virtually all of those sold commercially—the mapleleaf, three-ridge, ebony and washboard mussels.

There are still two ways of taking mussels—by hand and by brail, a sort of underwater rake towed by a boat. Since most commercially viable beds are in deep water, divers do the bulk of the hand harvesting. Often working with partners who keep an eye on air pumps in boats above, divers descend deep into waterways like Kentucky Lake, collecting sacksful of shells. It's dangerous work conducted in low-visibility conditions, often by untrained divers, and there were eight deaths in 1990 among the 2,300 divers in Tennessee's waters. That figure, though, was abnormally high, according to Robert Todd, a commercial fishing/musseling coordinator with the Tennessee Wildlife Resources Agency, who says one or two deaths a year is a more common number.

The shells are taken to dealers, with Tennessee Shell Co. being the largest. The company pays from 55 cents to $4.35 a pound, depending on the size and species of shell, and a good diver can make well over $200 a day. Shells are sorted, sacked, and shipped by truck to Memphis, where they are taken by rail to the West Coast and then by ship to Japan. TWRA estimated the statewide harvest of shells at 4,760 tons in 1990. It considered that figure too high to be sustainable, and introduced new size limits and other regulations that cut the 1991 harvest to about 2,400 tons.

Related and peripheral industries make the mussel business a $20 million per year industry. One of its key players is John Latendresse, who owns American Pearl Co., which designs and manufactures jewelry, selling to a clientele that includes Service Merchandise and Macy's. He also owns American Pearl Farms, the nation's only successful pearl-culturing operation, developed after years of painstaking work. Latendresse will harvest pearls from 500,000 shells this year. The companies are headquartered in Camden, where Latendresse, who also has the world's largest collection of fresh-water pearls, has done business since 1954.

Despite the classic success of all aspects of Tennessee's freshwater pearl business, daunting problems remain. Pollution, particularly from farm chemicals, has been a major problem on Kentucky Lake for years, and Latendresse lost hundreds of thousands of dollars when a portion of his mussel crop was wiped out in 1989. In many sections of the state, only a small percentage of the mussels found by divers are fit for sale. Even the colder-than-normal winter of 1994 had an effect, delaying mussel harvesting and damaging a portion of Latendresse's physical plant.

TWRA's Todd sees progress in the implementation of size limits and other measures, though.

"I think we have protected the mussels to assure they can at least attain a size at which they're capable of sexual reproduction," he said. "There is a lot of pressure on the resource; our best guess is that about 80 percent of what attains legal size in one year is removed. We're managing on the edge there, but we feel we've got the size limits large enough that our resource will be protected."

The agency has imposed sanctuaries in areas that contain rare mussels and, while poaching remains a problem, a fee charged buyers of shells has enabled TWRA to hire a mussel enforcement officer as well as a biologist and technician.

It remains to be seen whether those efforts can turn the tide in the effort to improve conditions for our most fragile state symbol, one extremely sensitive to the kinds of problems growth and pollution bring.

Rock: Agate

Agate has long held a fascination for mankind. Jewelry made from agate pebbles has been found in pre-dynastic Egyptian tombs and in ancient Roman ruins. Named for the Achates River (probably the current Drillo in Sicily), where it was found in abundance, this relatively common, widely distributed gemstone has long been used for adornment and in items ranging from cups and plates to holy water founts, knife handles and children's marbles.

Although Tennessee is not particularly rich in agate, and there is no commercial exploitation of the mineral here, the state's Legislature named agate the state rock in 1969, preceding by 10 years the naming of the more commonly known state rock, limestone. In fact, the great, slow processes that build and erode the earth's surface have bound the formation of agate with the erosion of limestone in Tennessee, and have left the state with a concentration of agate in the Wartrace area and with scatterings elsewhere.

Agate is a form of one of the most common substances on earth—silica, or silicon dioxide, a combination of the elements silicon and oxygen. Silica takes three forms—crystalline, known as quartz; amorphous, known as chert; and impure, known as sand. Agate is a form of chert, and differs from other forms simply in that it is ornamental; it often has a pleasing color because of impurities, usually trace metals, or attractive banded patterns because of the way it is formed.

That process begins when water, flowing through rocks at or near the earth's surface, dissolves a certain amount of the abundant silica found there. In many parts of the world, agates are formed within volcanic rock—ancient lavas—while in others, including Tennessee, they are formed in limestone, with much of the silica being supplied by sandstone. The silica travels with the groundwater, seeping through porous rock and being stopped or redirected by layers of harder rock. It remains in solution so long as the conditions under which it dissolved remain the same. If, however, it comes to a place where the pH, pressure or temperature changes sufficiently, it is deposited by means of precipitation, one thin layer at a time. This occurs most frequently along joints, which are cracks in rock beds, or in bedding planes, which mark the boundaries between adjacent layers of rock. This means the agate will often form in veins, or settle in pockets known as geodes, eroded holes which may range from the size of a fingernail to five or six feet across.

The precipitation that deposits agate is a slow, painstaking process that works from the outside in, forming concentric layers one at a time. If the process is interrupted or changed, the core of an agate will reflect that. The center can be made up of quartz if, for example, a more hurried precipitation takes over.

The difference between the agate found relatively abundantly in the Wartrace area and the much more sporadic agate found elsewhere in the state seems to be its source. The quartz veins cutting across some of the sedimentary rocks in the Wartrace area were deposited by water that was hotter than normal, and geologists speculate there may have been an igneous source for this heat, such as an ancient lava flow.

The agate found outside the Wartrace area is usually associated with a present or ancient stream bed. Water erodes limestone, exposing agate, which is washed into the stream. If a chunk remains in water long enough, the tumbling of the stream will smooth its rough edges and leave it in pebble form. Areas near Cookeville, Jellico, Memphis, Murfreesboro and Shelbyville are all sources of this type of agate.

There are several varieties of agate, characterized by differences in the shapes and colors of the bands that make them up. Those bands are exposed by cutting the rock in cross-section. In riband agate, the bands appear as straight lines. A ring or eye agate has concentric circular bands resembling one of its namesakes; these were once used to ward off "the evil eye." Moss agate contains green fibrous sections suggesting plant matter. When white bands alternate with bands of black, the stone is called onyx; with brown, sardonyx; and with red, carnelian or red agate. All three have been classically used in the making of cameos.

Agate is found throughout the world, with Brazil and Uruguay, central Europe, southern India and Malagasy, and the northwestern U.S. being particularly rich sources. Its abundance means it is regarded as "semi-precious," and even in the time of the Roman scholar Pliny the Elder, agate was inexpensive except for remarkably attractive specimens.

For all the rich beds throughout the world, though, only a small percentage of the agate found is gem quality. Much of it, therefore, is artificially colored in various processes involving heat, chemicals and radiation.

The other processing necessary is shaping. Agates are broken into pieces approximating the shape of the end product, then ground and polished with various tools. Small pieces are used in jewelry, and larger pieces in a variety of objects, including mortars and pestles, candlesticks, inkstands, blotters and clock faces.

Despite the lack of formal commercial use of Tennessee agate, collectors come from great distances to collect it here, and some are no doubt amateur cutters who sell some of what they fashion from the stones. They are among the true appreciators of the slowly formed rock that is one of Tennessee's most colorful state symbols.

Rock: Limestone

It was the last day of February 1979, and one of the most intensive lobbying campaigns in the annals of Tennessee politics was about to come to fruition. The lobbyists themselves jammed the gallery of the state House, which was debating their measure, House Bill 494. Every member of both the House and Senate had been contacted, and some of the most powerful political figures in the state had been recruited to spearhead the bill's passage—House Speaker Ned

Ray McWherter and Senate Majority Leader Senator Milton Hamilton, Jr. among them.

One measure of the campaign's success was the fact that the Senate had earlier passed the measure 30-0, and its passage in the House was considered a *fait accompli*. Sure enough, the final vote was 91-0, and the lobbyists—148 sixth-grade students from Martin Junior High School in Weakley County—cheered wildly. Governor Lamar Alexander would sign the bill into law March 13th, and Tennessee would have a new addition to its group of state symbols—a state rock, limestone.

The students, under their teacher, Mrs. Wilbur ("Miss Jenny") Vaughan, had been studying state symbols during their Tennessee history class, and discovered there was no state rock listed. (Agate had, in fact, been named 10 years earlier in a House resolution, but the measure was never passed into law; it is now recognized as a state rock.) During the several months they spent campaigning, they learned a great deal about not only limestone and the inner workings of government, but also the news media, for there was a great deal of press coverage.

In lobbying for official recognition of limestone, Miss Jenny and her students focused attention on an important economic commodity, a valuable building material, and a priceless scientific and historical treasure, one that tells us a great deal about the Tennessee history that stretches back hundreds of millions of years before the arrival of even the first Native Americans. And since it underlies the entire state, with outcrops throughout Middle and Eastern Tennessee, they were sure it would be acceptable to all three of the state's grand geographical divisions.

The only real competition for state rock among the students had been marble, another important commodity in the Volunteer State, but a little study resolved even that dilemma. Marble *is* limestone, crystallized by heat and pressure.

Limestone is a sedimentary rock comprised primarily of

Aubrey Watson

Tennessee's capitol sits atop a limestone bed, visible here between sections of its retaining wall. The bed is part of the Cathys formation, which lies just above the Bigby limestone quarried a few blocks away for construction of the capitol.

calcium carbonate, which is deposited on shallow sea floors over long periods of time. The calcium carbonate comes from various sources. One is from simple surface run-off: rain dissolves some of the mineral, which is carried by rivers to the sea, where it settles to the bottom. Another is from direct precipitation in seawater, whereby chemical processes cause it to settle out. A third is biochemical: coral and other hard shells secreted by animals gradually sink and become part of a limestone layer. It is this process that gives us so many of the fossils prized by paleontologists and other scientists. These three processes can occur singly or in combination, with bits of shell and debris tossed and ground up by currents, then piled on the sea floor, and loose grains squeezed together and cemented by pressure over a long period of time in a process known as lithification.

Throughout the earth's long history, the region that is now Tennessee has been at the whim of the same massive geological forces that have shaped the rest of the earth's surface and substrata—the rising and falling of oceans, the weathering and re-building of mountains, and the folding, crushing, heating and cooling of rock. A little less than 600 million years ago, seas were advancing over Tennessee, so that much of the state was part of a continental shelf not unlike the present-day Caribbean. Corals were being built, with carbonates from surface run-off and from chemical precipitation settling to the bottom and being used for shell-building by aquatic creatures. All would become part of a huge layer of limestone that underlies the state. That layer varies from 2,500 feet thick in East Tennessee to over a mile thick in Stewart County along Kentucky Lake. Then, perhaps 500 million years ago, the seas retreated and surface weathering began. Since limestone is highly soluble in slightly acidic groundwater, this was a period during which many caves and sinkholes were formed. Slow drips from the ceilings of such caves became responsible in many places for the limestone formations known as stalactites and stalagmites.

A new advance of oceans tens of millions of years later brought thick mud sediments that would become shale in East Tennessee, but Middle Tennessee again saw the formation of lime deposits in its shallow ocean water. This was the Ordovician period, from 500 million to 430 million years ago, and it is responsible for fossil-rich beds called, in part, the Stones River Group and the Nashville Group. They lie beneath much of the central portion of the state, a 600-foot-deep limestone basin which is actually the weathered remnant of a massive natural dome. The Ordovician period saw the formation of rock layers that give us much of the limestone needed in the state for construction, cement and agriculture. These layers contain some of the world's most important zinc deposits. In the central basin, they're mined for phosphates, and in the East they're quarried for high-quality commercial marble.

Iron found in seawater sometimes replaced lime shells and lime mud in sufficient quantities that it would later be mined in Tennessee, with the mining and processing of ore responsible for the establishment and growth of communities like Rockwood, Dayton, Cumberland Gap, LaFollette and Ross's Landing (now Chattanooga). In many parts of the state, chimneys from furnaces used for smelting are still standing.

During the making of steel, lime obtained from limestone is used as flux to promote fusion, one of its many commercial and industrial uses. Others include the making of toothpaste, paints, chemicals, whitewash, bleaching powder and glass. Several fungicides are made with lime, and it's used in some medicines, in water purification, and in the paper industry. It's also used in lithography and is a catalyst in the plant fertilization process.

One of the most visible and historic uses of limestone is in building. Tennessee's capitol, to take one well-known example, was originally constructed of limestone from a nearby quarry, and the interior was faced with native marble from East Tennessee. The exterior had deteriorated badly by the late 1950s and was replaced by Indiana limestone.

Crushed limestone has a number of important building uses as well. It's mixed with asphalt to make blacktop, it's used as gravel for roads and driveways, and it's a basic natural component of portland cement, so it's part of all concrete.

Overall, there is no state symbol as pervasive in our day-to-day lives as limestone. We drive on it, we work surrounded by it, we use products made with it, and we eat food it helps to grow. Small wonder that Miss Jenny and her sixth-graders at Martin Junior High School kicked off the campaign that gave limestone its official statewide recognition.

Tennessee Photographic Services

Songs and Poem

If you've ever heard the University of Tennessee marching band strike up "Rocky Top" before 95,000 delirious fans in Knoxville's Neyland Stadium, you've been witness to the soul-stirring power of a state song.

"Rocky Top," which had been used at UT football and basketball games for years as an unofficial anthem and rabble-rouser, wasn't made an official state song until 1982, when it became the fifth (yes, fifth) song so honored. It

joined, according to *Nashville Banner* writer Michael
Erickson, "the formerly sedate coterie of official state songs,"
which included "My Homeland, Tennessee," "When It's Iris
Time In Tennessee," "My Tennessee," and "Tennessee
Waltz." Counting two state bicentennial songs and a very
popular precursor to the official canon, you can see that the
Volunteer State's reputation as a music center is not without
political merit.

On the surface, "Rocky Top" doesn't appear to have the
classical qualifications for a state song. It is, after all, a tribute
to a mountain life where corn liquor and an occasional murder
aren't unheard of, and where nostalgia is more likely to turn
toward a girl who's "wild as a mink" than toward the statue
on the town square. It's that very spirit of mountain wildness,
though, that gives "Rocky Top" its stirring quality. The song,
written in 1967 by Felice and Boudleaux Bryant, who were
responsible for a large number of hits, including many of the
Everly Brothers' classic recordings, is as popular nationwide
as it is in Tennessee. Since first being committed to vinyl by
the Osborne Brothers, it has been recorded more than 100
times by other artists.

The saga of the Volunteer State's wealth of state songs
actually begins in 1897. It was a year late, but Tennessee was
celebrating the centennial of its admission to the Union.
Organizers needed a state flag to fly during the celebration,
and they adopted one that quickly fell into disuse [See
Chapter 1]. They also wanted a song to sing at the May 1st
grand opening, and they selected "Tennessee," which had
been written by A. J. Holt to the tune of the old hymn "Beulah
Land." In the 1920s, in a pamphlet called *Tennessee: State
Flag-Flower-Song Etc.*, State Librarian John Trotwood Moore
said of "Tennessee," "While not legally adopted by the
Legislature, public sentiment has very generally made it the
State Song." Moore reprinted it, but wrote a second chorus,
"that the song might have its proper atmosphere of Tennessee
history."

The state Legislature first decided to designate an official state song in 1925, and the work chosen was "My Homeland, Tennessee." It had been a poem by Nell Grayson Taylor, and Nebraska native Roy Lamont Smith set it to music while a member of the faculty of the Cadek Conservatory of Music in Chattanooga.

In 1935, the Legislature honored a song sung in praise of another state symbol, the iris. "When It's Iris Time In Tennessee" had been written by Willa Mae Waid and was, according to press reports at the time, used extensively in school pageants during Iris Festival Week.

It took 20 years for the next addition to Tennessee's official musical family. In 1955, "My Tennessee," written by Frances Hannah Tranum of Johnson City, was adopted as the official state public school song. Then, in 1965, the Legislature turned to a more widely known song, one that had been on the national charts in the '40s. "Tennessee Waltz," the Redd Stewart-Pee Wee King chestnut, finally gave the state a song that much of the population would know. In fact, it's still widely considered *the* Tennessee state song, and some publications, including *The World Almanac*, list it as such.

The approach of the nation's 200th birthday celebration in 1976 spurred Tennessee's legislators to recognize two more songs, this time as state bicentennial songs. They gave the nod in 1975 to "The Tennessee Salute," written by the state's poet laureate, Richard M. "Pek" Gunn, and a year later to "Fly Eagle, Fly" by James Rogers.

In 1992, the Legislature adopted "Tennessee" by Vivian Rorie as official song of the 97th General Assembly. The 1991-1994 edition of the *Tennessee Blue Book* lists the composition as a state song, but it is not.

Could it happen again? Is there a chance that the Volunteer State's incredible musical riches could produce another song deemed appropriate to serve in an official capacity? We'll just have to wait and see.

On the following pages, Tennessee's state songs:

Tennessee

The land of pure and balmy air,
Of streams so clear and skies so fair,
Of mountains grand and fountains free,
The lovely land of Tennessee.

First Chorus:
Oh, Tennessee, fair Tennessee,
The land of all the world to me;
I stand upon thy mountains high
And hold communion with the sky,
And view the glowing landscape o'er,
Old Tennessee forevermore.

The fairest of the fair we see,
The bravest of the brave have we,
The freest of the noble free,
In Liberty-loving Tennessee.

Second Chorus:
Oh Tennessee, brave Tennessee,
King's Mountain called you to be free,
From Chalmette's plain to Mexico
Your loyal sons were first to go,
When Freedom calls, though far or near,
Old Tennessee is Volunteer.

The rarest fruits and fairest flowers,
And happiest homes on earth are ours,
If heaven below could only be,
'Twould surely shine in Tennessee.

Repeat First Chorus

Awake my harp with tuneful string,

And of thy lovely country sing,
From east to west, the chorus be,
God bless our Dear Old Tennessee.

Repeat Second Chorus

by A. J. Holt (Air, "Beulah Land"). Second chorus by John Trotwood Moore.

Tennessee Photographic Services

My Homeland, Tennessee

O Tennessee, that gave us birth,
To thee our hearts bow down.
For thee our love and loyalty
Shall weave a fadeless crown.
Thy purple hills our cradle was;
Thy fields our mother breast
Beneath thy sunny bended skies,
Our childhood days were blessed.

Chorus:
O Tennessee: Fair Tennessee:
Our love for thee can never die:
Dear homeland, Tennessee.

'Twas long ago our fathers came,
A free and noble band,
Across the mountain's frowning heights
To seek a promised land.
And here before their raptured eyes;
In beauteous majesty:
Outspread the smiling valleys
Of the winding Tennessee.

Could we forget our heritage
Of heroes strong and brave?
Could we do aught but cherish it,
Unsullied to the grave?
Ah no! the State where Jackson sleeps,
Shall ever peerless be.
We glory in thy majesty;
Our homeland, Tennessee.

Words by Nell Grayson Taylor. Music by Roy Lamont Smith.

When It's Iris Time In Tennessee

Sweetness of Spring memories bring
Of a place I long to be.
Land of Sunshine calls this old heart of mine,
Come back to Tennessee.

Chorus:
When it's Iris time down in Tennessee,
I'll be coming back to stay
Where the mockingbird sings at the break of day
A lilting love song gay.
Where the iris grows,
Where the Harpeth flows,
That is where I long to be.
There's a picture there that lives in memory
When it's Iris time in Tennessee.

by Willa Mae Waid

My Tennessee

Beloved state, oh state of mine,
In all the world I could not find,
Where God has strewn with lavish hand,
More natural beauty o'er the land.
From ev'ry stream and valley green
His wond'rous art is ever seen.
Ah, let my heart beat true to thee,
And swell with pride for Tennessee.

Chorus:
Oh, Tennessee, My Tennessee,
Thy hills and vales are fair to see,
With mountains grand, and fertile lands
There is no state more dear to me.
Thro' other climes tho I may roam,
There will be times I'll long for home,
In Tennessee, Fair Tennessee,
The land of my nativity.

Thy rocks and rills, and wooded hills,
My mem'ry keeps the childhood thrills
You gave to me, that I might know
The joys supreme, you could bestow.
The song of birds, the whisp'ring trees,
The low of herds, the hum of bees,
It all comes back so dear to me,
My childhood home in Tennessee.

Your battles fought and vict'ries won,
Your freedom bought and duty done,
With daughters fair, and sons so brave,
To do and dare, their deeds they gave
Courageously, without a fear
And won the name of volunteer

In sacred trust, let those who will,
By being just, preserve it still.

by Frances Hannah Tranum

Tennessee Photographic Services

Tennessee Waltz

I was waltzing with my darlin' to the Tennessee Waltz
When an old friend I happened to see
Introduced him to my loved one and while they were waltzing
My friend stole my sweetheart from me.

I remember the night and the Tennessee Waltz
Now I know just how much I have lost
Yes I lost my little darlin' the night they were playing
The beautiful Tennessee Waltz.

Rocky Top

Wish that I was on ol' Rocky Top,
Down in the Tennessee hills;
Ain't no smoggy smoke on Rocky Top,
Ain't no telephone bills.
Once I had a girl on Rocky Top,
Half bear, other half cat;
Wild as a mink, but sweet as soda pop,
I still dream about that.

Chorus:
Rocky Top, you'll always be
Home sweet home to me;
Good ol' Rocky Top;
Rocky Top, Tennessee;
Rocky Top, Tennessee.

Once two strangers climbed ol' Rocky Top,
Lookin' for a moonshine still;
Strangers ain't come down from Rocky Top,
Reckon they never will;
Corn don't grow at all on Rocky Top,
Dirt's too rocky by far;
That's why all the folks on Rocky Top
Get their corn from a jar.

I've had years of cramped-up city life
Trapped like a duck in a pen;
All I know is it's a pity life
Can't be simple again.

by Boudleaux and Felice Bryant
© Copyright 1967 by House of Bryant Publications
Used by Permission.

The Tennessee Salute

Tennessee, oh how I love you
With your fertile rolling plain
Purple tinted hills and mountains
Tow-ring over fields of grain

Smoke and steam from busy fact'ries
Rising upward in the air
From the Smoky Mountains to the Mississippi
Happiness is ev'rywhere

Tennessee, your lakes are playgrounds
Where the water skiers sway
To the speeding boats that pull them
Through the misty silv'ry spray

Trout and bream and bass and crappie
Finest in the U.S.A.
When you go a-fishin', catch instead of wishin'
Hurrah for the good ole TVA

Tennessee, oh how I love you
There is none that is above you
You are on the move
Tennessee is on the double
With a minimum of trouble
No one could disprove

Tennessee is on good footing
Industry is really putting
Hard times on the run
If ev'rything that's done and said
Puts good ole Tennessee ahead
We'll all join in the fun

Words and music by Richard M. "Pek" Gunn
© Richard M. "Pek" Gunn

Fly, Eagle, Fly

Today I saw an eagle flying
The colors, they were red and white and blue
Today it looked like he was crying
For where are all the friends that once he knew?

Chorus:
And I said, Fly, Eagle, Fly!
Go spread your freedom wings across the sky
Don't let 'em bring you down
They'll chain you to the ground
You gotta be strong to travel alone in the sky
So Fly, Eagle, Fly!

Today I heard the eagle calling
It echoed from the mountains to the sea
But, again, the lonely sounds he made were falling
Upon the deafened ears of those not free

Repeat Chorus

Today I saw an eagle flying
Is he headed for the skies he's never known?
Are the freedoms he has left behind him dying?
Will the eagle find another home?

Repeat Chorus

by James Rogers
© 1975 by James Rogers

The state poem, "Oh Tennessee, My Tennessee," was officially adopted in 1973 by the 88th General Assembly.

Oh Tennessee, My Tennessee

Oh Tennessee, my Tennessee
What love and pride I feel for thee.
You proud ole state, the volunteer,
Your proud traditions I hold dear.

I revere your heroes
Who bravely fought our country's foes.
Renowned statesmen, so wise and strong,
Who served our country well and long.

I thrill at thought of mountains grand;
Rolling green hills and fertile farm land;
Earth rich with stone, mineral and ore;
Forests dense and wild flowers galore;

Powerful rivers that bring us light;
Deep lakes with fish and fowl in flight;
Thriving cities and industries;
Fine schools and universities;

Strong folks of pioneer descent,
Simple, honest, and reverent.
Beauty and hospitality
Are the hallmarks of Tennessee.

And o'er the world as I may roam,
No place exceeds my boyhood home.
And oh how much I long to see
My native land, my Tennessee.

by Admiral William Lawrence

*Square dancers Gene Edwards and Janie Selby,
banjo player Bruce Weathers, fiddler John Hagar
and guitarist Al Register.*

Folk Dance: Square Dance

Gene Edwards' love for square dancing started simply enough. "It looked like clean fun and I just got interested," he says. What began as a way to spend a little free time, though, has become a long-term passion for Edwards, whose square dance team, The Dixieland Dancers, takes the high energy and precision of square dancing (which has been designated the Tennessee state folk dance) to audiences both in and out of the Volunteer State.

Square dancing has thousands of adherents in Tennessee, dancing in converted stores and skating rinks, in barns, on outdoor platforms and on the stage of Nashville's Grand Ole Opry. In doing so, they're taking part in a tradition that can be traced for hundreds of years to the courts and countrysides of Europe, and which continues to be, according to Edwards, "good entertainment, good exercise, and a good way to get out of the house and forget your problems for awhile."

The Dixieland Dancers dance regularly at events like Nashville's Summer Lights Festival, at county fairs, bluegrass festivals and fiddlers' jamborees, and at fund-raisers for everything from local volunteer fire departments to the American Heart Association. They've also danced at the Opryland Hotel, at Twitty City, at events in Georgia and North Carolina, and, in a grand example of musical ambassadorship, for representatives of Hendersonville's sister city, Tsuru, Japan.

Square dancing can be traced to two European dances: the cotillion, one of the fashionable dances of the French court that dominated Western Europe's aristocratic ballrooms in the 17th and 18th centuries, and the English country dances, fashionable among the common people. There were many types of the latter, including the contra, for a double file of couples, and the round dance, for a circle of dancers. One of the forms into which the round dance evolved was the Kentucky running set, a complicated figure dance. Social events often saw a mixing of dance styles, and square dancing evolved as a sort of combination of the Kentucky running set and the cotillion. Modern square dancing reflects the influence of buckdancing as well.

Square dances came with European immigrants to America, and became a staple of rural and town life alike, often being held by farmers as part of corn husking bees. The "square" in square dancing is formed by four couples, who begin and end the dance in that figure, facing each other. To accompaniment that generally includes fiddle, guitar, banjo and bass, they execute ordered patterns that involve a number of steps, the exchange of partners, circling and the like, under the direction of a caller (callers were introduced to square dancing in the 19th century). In Western Swing square dancing, the caller has a microphone, is generally not one of the dancers, and often improvises as the dance progresses. In the type done by the Dixieland Dancers and many other Tennessee groups, the calling is done by one of the dancers, and may reflect a routine worked out in advance. The promenade (moving counter-clockwise in a circle) and do-si-do (passing shoulder-to-shoulder and circling back-to-back) are among the more familiar patterns. Others have names like shooting the star, bird in the cage, rock the cradle, four-leaf clover and double shoo-fly sway.

There is much more to what Edwards and his group do than is apparent from the dancing itself. "When we're in North Carolina or somewhere dancing," he says, "we're not just promoting square dancing; we're promoting Tennessee as well."

There's also the matter of the dance's tradition and heritage, something Edwards would very much like to keep alive. Commenting on other popular forms of dancing, like the Texas Two-Step, he says, "I'd just hate to see them take the place of Tennessee's traditional dances completely."

While groups like the Dixieland Dancers can make it look easy, anyone who's tried it can tell you that becoming proficient at square dancing takes some practice. The rewards, though, in terms of fun, exercise, and socialization, have prompted thousands of Tennesseans to join in.

The rewards sometimes go much farther than that. At a square dance held at a converted skating rink in Lebanon, Edwards pointed to a boy about 14 who was learning the steps.

"See that boy?" he asked. "He could be out somewhere getting into drinking or drugs. Instead, he's here doing this and having fun at it. I think that's great."

State Seal

For all of Tennessee's state symbols, there is only one that could be considered vital to the day-to-day operation of government. The state did quite well for almost two centuries without a state insect, fish, rock or butterfly; for nearly a century and a half without a bird or song; for almost a century without an official flag; and for nearly half a century without even a permanent capitol.

The state seal, though, is another story. There was one in

the works before Tennessee was admitted to the union, and though it wasn't actually delivered and used until 1802— nearly six years after statehood was achieved—the Great Seal of the State of Tennessee is without doubt the Volunteer State's oldest symbol and the one most closely associated with its daily functioning.

Seals have long been used with the official documents of royalty and government to guarantee authenticity and, formerly, privacy. They were originally used to make impressions in sealing wax but are now generally pressed onto foil or the document itself, and though they have long been replaced by the signature as an authenticating mark, they are still used widely as official symbols.

The first mention of a seal for the state came with the adoption of Tennessee's constitution in February 1796. Article II, Section 15, said, "There shall be a seal of this state, which shall be kept by the governor, and used by him officially, and shall be called 'the great seal of the state of Tennessee.' " The second mention came when the Legislature outlined, on April 20, 1796, the duties of the secretary of state. "The governor," the act states, "shall cause a seal of this state to be provided: and copies of records and papers in the said office authenticated under said seal, shall be evidence equally as the original record or paper."

Just five days later, Governor John Sevier wrote to the state's U.S. senators, William Blount and William Cocke, who were attending to their official duties in Philadelphia: "There being no proper artist (in my opinion) in this State competent to the completion of a seal that might be considered and thought sufficient....I take the liberty to request that our Senators will take the trouble on themselves to have a suitable seal made, and provided, at the expense of the State...as will be elegant, comprehensive and sufficiently expressive of the purposes and use the same is intended for."

Blount and Cocke were apparently unable to comply with the request, and Dr. R. L. C. White, speaking before the

Tennessee Historical Society in 1900, speculated that they probably simply didn't have the time. Congress would adjourn in 30 days, "and in the press of more important business, and the harassment consequent upon the uncertainty as to the admission of the state [it would become official on June 1], they no doubt neglected to have the seal made."

Sevier, then, did the only thing he could do. He stamped state documents with his personal seal. His successor, Governor Archibald Roane, did likewise. No one in the new state's government undertook to remedy the situation until September 26, 1801, when the fourth General Assembly appointed a joint committee "to contract with a suitable per-

Left, the state seal as designed in 1801; right, the current seal.

son to cut a seal and make a press for this state."

There is, unfortunately, no record of who designed the seal, but on November 14 the committee returned with a design. The Senate journal reported its recommendation that "the said seal be a circle, two inches and a quarter in diameter; that the circumference of the circle contain the words, 'The great seal of Tennessee,' that in the lower part of said circumference be inserted 'February 6, 1796,' the date of the constitution of this state; that in the inside of the upper part of said circle be set in numerical letters 'XVI,' the number of the state in chronological order; that under the base of the upper semicircle there be the word 'Agriculture'; that above said base there be the figure of a plough, sheaf of wheat and cotton plant; that in the lower part of the lower semicircle there be the word 'Commerce'; and said lower semicircle shall also contain the figure of a boat and boatman."

William and Matthew Atkinson of Knoxville were contracted to cut the seal and make a press for it, as well as to keep both in repair "so long as either of them reside in this state." They delivered it to Roane, and it was first used on April 24, 1802, on the document authorizing their payment of $100. The only variation from the committee's specifications was the addition of the words 'the state of' to the words on the seal's circumference.

The first in a series of modifications of the seal took place in 1829, during the administration of Governor William Carroll. This second seal was one and three-quarters inches in diameter, with the plow, wheat, cotton and boat redrawn, and "February 6" dropped from the date at the bottom. The change was apparently made without official legislative action.

Yet another seal was used briefly in 1865, during the administration of William Brownlow. It was replaced in 1866 by two seals quite similar to each other—one of which is the seal still in use by the state. It received official adoption in 1987 by the 95th General Assembly. The current seal drops the boatman from the boat and again updates the visual elements, but is otherwise true to the original design.

There are three seals and presses currently in the capitol. A large press, probably mid-Victorian, according to state museum curator of art and architecture Jim Hoobler, holds the seal in the governor's outer office. A much smaller table-top press, probably dating from the turn of the century, holds the seal in the outer office of the secretary of state, to the left as you enter. There is a still smaller press holding an older version of the seal to the right in that office.

None of these, however, is used regularly for official documents, as the process of hand-pressing each one is extraordinarily time-consuming, especially with a state that uses about 100,000 a year. By contrast, Oklahoma may use 10,000 a year, and Arizona 25,000. Instead, Tennessee contracts to have pre-stamped, peel-off gold foil seals made to attach to special documents.

If that seems to lessen the mystique surrounding them somewhat, that's as it should be, according to Dale Conner of the J. T. Lovell company, which supplies them to the state.

"If you happen to get ahold of a seal, there's nothing about it that's going to allow you to do anything," he says. "You can't get a prisoner out of jail or get someone in Treasury to cut you a check. It takes a lot more than a gold seal to do that. They're decorations, basically."

As such, the seal's design is used in a number of other ways. It adorns the sides of some state vehicles, and various state officials have had the seal put on coasters, umbrellas, pens, binders, glassware and lapel pins. All such proposed items go through the state's system of approvals, and those contracted to make them are advised simply to keep items "in good taste," according to Conner.

There are, in addition, two painted representations of the seal on ceilings in the capitol. One is in the governor's outer office above the press and seal itself, and the other is on the ceiling in the foyer near the Sixth Avenue entrance. This one is regularly pointed out on tours of the capitol, particularly since the legends Agriculture and Commerce, and their accompanying representations, are in reversed positions.

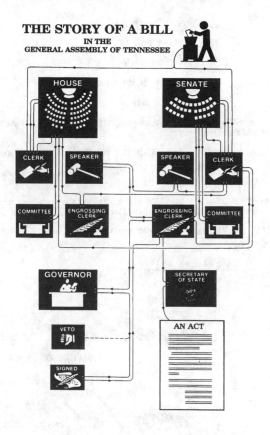

THE STORY OF A BILL
IN THE
GENERAL ASSEMBLY OF TENNESSEE

How We Get State Symbols—
The Legislative Process

Whatever its initial impetus, a state symbol is a product of the Tennessee Legislature. The bill naming it must, like all other bills, go through a committee system, receive the approval of both houses and be signed by the governor.

The process that gets a bill introduced in the first place,

PUBLIC CHAPTER NO. 896

SENATE BILL NO. 1772

By Wright

Substituted for: House Bill No. 2187

By Stamps

AN ACT To amend Tennessee Code Annotated, Title 4, Chapter 1, Part 3, relative to the official state butterfly.

BE IT ENACTED BY THE GENERAL ASSEMBLY OF THE STATE OF TENNESSEE:

SECTION 1. Tennessee Code Annotated, Title 4, Chapter 1, Part 3, is amended by adding a new section as follows:

Section 4-1-319. The beautiful zebra swallowtail, Eurytides marcellus, is hereby designated as the official state butterfly.

SECTION 2. This act shall take effect upon becoming a law, the public welfare requiring it.

PASSED: _____ April 19, 1994 _____

_____

JOHN S. WILDER,
SPEAKER OF THE SENATE

_____

JIMMY NAIFEH, SPEAKER
HOUSE OF REPRESENTATIVES

APPROVED this ___9___ day of ___May___ 1994

_____

NED McWHERTER, GOVERNOR

though, can vary widely. Some of the stories behind various symbols are outlined in this book, but it's worthwhile now to take a close-up look at how one symbol went from idea to official status. We'll look at the most recent, as of this writing, the state butterfly.

The story begins at Calloway Gardens, a family resort outside Atlanta boasting golf courses, natural areas and the Cecil B. Day Butterfly Center, an enclosed facility featuring more than 500 species of butterflies. Mrs. Sherrill Charlton, who teaches biology and chemistry at Tennessee's Gallatin High School, was on vacation with her family there in 1993.

"They hold workshops," she said, "and I was attending one where they gave out a sheet listing which states have state butterflies. Tennessee didn't, and I thought it would be neat for us to have one."

She approached State Senator Don Wright, who represents her Sumner/Robertson County senatorial district, and said she'd like to have her students select an appropriate butterfly to be added to the list of state symbols. He said he'd be glad to help and urged her to get other schools in the community involved.

The state Legislature began its 1994 session on January 11 and, to assure the matter would be considered during the upcoming session, Wright asked the Legislature's Legal Services Department to draft a bill naming the monarch state butterfly, with the understanding that the actual butterfly selected would be substituted before the bill came to a final vote. He asked Representative Randy Stamps of Hendersonville to sponsor the bill in the House.

In the meantime, Mrs. Charlton sent a letter to every school in Sumner County, asking for input toward finding "the best representative butterfly in Tennessee."

"This will not solve the world hunger problem, decide how to make up snow days or lower taxes," she told them,

Opposite: the signed 1994 bill making the zebra swallowtail Tennessee's state butterfly.

"but it is an opportunity for our students to become involved in the working of state government."

Senator Wright submitted the bill to the Senate clerk's office, which attached a number to it, making it Senate Bill 1772. In the House, Representative Stamps submitted the same bill to the House clerk, creating House Bill 2187. The measures joined 2,400 other pieces of legislation under consideration.

In the Senate, the bill passed on first and second reading, then entered the committee system. On February 1, Senator Wright wrote Mrs. Charlton:

"I brought SB 1772 before the Senate State And Local Government Committee this morning. It passed unanimously by a vote of 9-0 and has been sent onto the full Senate with a recommendation for passage . . . I look forward to your class completing its decision on which butterfly to use and will keep the bill off the calendar until after your decision."

Finally, on February 17, after Mrs. Charlton's students had weighed the responses from other schools, considered the candidates and made their final selection, the bill reached the floor of the Senate. It was treated there with the mixture of seriousness and levity so often characteristic of the state Legislature.

The first order of business was the amendment replacing the monarch with the students' choice, the zebra swallowtail, a decidedly less-familiar butterfly.

"I'm just shocked," said Senator Bob Rochelle of Lebanon, "that the senator from Sumner has turned his back on the beautiful monarch."

Senator Stephen Cohen of Memphis followed in a more serious vein with a motion to refer the bill back to committee, since, he said, it "thought the monarch has significance to Tennessee."

An amended motion, to send the bill to the Judiciary Committee, prompted Senator Bud Gilbert of Knoxville to quip, "Mr. Speaker, we can't do that, because the whole pur-

pose of this bill is to preserve the butterfly. If we send it to
Judiciary, it will become extinct."

The motion to send it to Judiciary failed 18-12, and the
motion to send it to State and Local Government failed 22-7.
The initial amendment, to replace the monarch with the zebra
swallowtail, passed 26-4. The bill now read as follows:

AN ACT to amend Tennessee Code Annotated, Title 4,
Chapter 1, Part 3, relative to the official state butterfly.
BE IT ENACTED BY THE GENERAL ASSEMBLY OF
THE STATE OF TENNESSEE:
SECTION 1. Tennessee Code Annotated, Title 4, Chapter
1, Part 3, is amended by adding a new section as follows:
Section 4-1-319. The beautiful zebra swallowtail,
Eurytides marcellus, is hereby designated as the official state
butterfly.
SECTION 2. This act shall take effect upon becoming a
law, the public welfare requiring it.

Senator Ray Albright of Harrison wanted reassurance that
the zebra swallowtail was, in fact, a Tennessee butterfly. He
received it, the question was called, and it passed 28-2.

That still left the House. Once Representative Stamps had
submitted it, House Bill 2187 passed the whole chamber on
two readings, then went to the State and Local Government
Committee and its State Government Subcommittee. It passed
both unanimously, then was placed on the House calendar by
the Calendar and Rules Committee.

It came before the full House on April 19 and faced the
same combination of concern and levity.

"If the mockingbird [the state bird] eats this butterfly,"
asked Representative Charles Severance of Knoxville, to
great laughter, "is there some kind of penalty?"

Representative Joe Bell of Lebanon expressed concern
that the addition of another insect symbol might diminish the
value of the state agricultural insect, the honeybee, and he

moved that the bill be referred to the Agriculture Committee for further study.

"This bill," countered Representative Stamps, "has been through the proper channels. It's been assigned through the committee system, through the subcommittee system, and a great deal of research has gone into the selection of this particular butterfly, so, with all due respect to the chairman, I will make a motion to table that motion to re-refer to the committee."

The tabling motion passed 44-41, bringing the original motion to a vote, and, by a margin of 63-19, with 13 not voting, the House approved the zebra swallowtail.

With approval by both houses, the bill was sent by the Senate Engrossing Clerk to Governor Ned Ray McWherter, who signed it into law on May 9, making it an official part of Tennessee statute and a permanent part of the state's heritage. Mrs. Charlton and her students had their part in making state history.

Aubrey Watson

The cupola of the state capitol.

BIBLIOGRAPHY

OVERALL

Crawford, Charles W. *Dynamic Tennessee: Land, History, and Government.* Austin: Steck-Vaughn, 1990.

Encyclopaedia Britannica. 32 vols. Chicago: Encyclopaedia Britannica, 1985.

Moore, John Trotwood. *Tennessee State Flag, Flower, Song, Seal, and Capitol,* 1922.

Reid, George K. *Pond Life: A Guide to Common Plants and Animals of North American Ponds and Lakes*. New York: Golden, 1987.

Tennessee Blue Book. Nashville: Secretary of State, 1991-94.

Tennessee State Library & Archives. Audio records of legislative functions.

Webster's Ninth New Collegiate Dictionary. Springfield: Merriam-Webster, 1991.

FLAG

Cannon, Devereaux D. *Flags of Tennessee*. Gretna: Pelican, 1990.

Madaus, Howard Michael. *The Battle Flags of the Confederate Army of Tennessee*. Milwaukee: Milwaukee Public Museum, 1976.

CAPITOL

Dardis, George. *Description of the plan, structure, and apartments of the state capitol of Tennessee*. Nashville: G. C. Torbett, 1855.

Gadski, Mary Ellen. "The Tennessee State Capitol: An Architectural History," *Tennessee Historical Quarterly*, Summer, 1988.

Ewing, James. *A Treasury of Tennessee Tales*. Nashville: Rutledge Hill, 1985.

Foster Lillian. *The state capitol*. Nashville, 1860.

Stromquist, Victor H. "Building and Restoration of the State Capitol." Address by Victor H. Stromquist, A.I.A., to Tennessee Historical Society, March 10, 1959.

Tennessee's Capitol. Filmstrip. Academy Learning Resources. Nashville: Film-Maker Productions in cooperation with the Metropolitan Nashville-Davidson County Board of Education, 1975.

MOCKINGBIRD, BOBWHITE QUAIL

Austin, Oliver L., Jr., and Arthur Singer. *Birds of the World*. New York: Golden, 1961.

Bierly, Michael Lee. *Bird Finding In Tennessee*. Nashville: Bierly, 1980.

Brauning, Daniel W., ed. *Atlas of Breeding Birds in Pennsylvania*. Pittsburgh: University of Pittsburgh Press, 1992.

Bull, John, Edith Bull, Gerald Gold, and Pieter D. Prall. *Birds of North America:* Eastern Region. Macmillan Field Guides. New York: Macmillan, 1985.

Bull, John, and John Farrand, Jr. *The Audobon Society Field Guide to North American Birds*: Eastern Region. New York: Knopf, 1977.

Burke, Ken, ed. (1983). *How To Attract Birds.* San Francisco: Ortho Books, 1983.

Burton, Robert. *Bird Behavior.* New York: Knopf, 1985.

————. *Bird Flight.* New York: Facts On File, 1990.

Campbell, Bruce. *The Dictionary of Birds in Color.* New York: Viking, 1974.

————, and Elizabeth Lack, eds. *A Dictionary of Birds.* Vermillion, SD: Buteo, 1985.

Cassidy, James, ed. *Reader's Digest Book of North American Birds.* Pleasantville: Reader's Digest, 1990.

Choate, Ernest A. *The Dictionary of American Bird Names.* Boston: Harvard Common Press, 1985.

Eriksson, Paul S., and Alan Pistorius. *Treasury of North American Bird Lore.* Middlebury, VT: Eriksson, 1987.

Erlich, Paul R., David S. Dobkoin, and Darryl Wheye. *The Birder's Handbook.* New York: Simon & Schuster, 1988.

Farrand, John, Jr., ed. *The Audobon Society Master Guide to Birding.* New York: Knopf, 1983.

Gruson, Edward S. *Words for Birds. A Lexicon of North American Birds with Biographical Notes.* New York: Quadrangle, 1972.

Harrison, Hal H. *A Field Guide to Birds' Nests.* Peterson Field Guide Series. Boston: Houghton Mifflin, 1975.

Headstrom, Richard. *A Complete Field Guide to Nests in the United States.* New York: Ives Washburn, 1970.

Imhof, Thomas A. *Alabama Birds.* State of Alabama Dept. of Conservation, 1962.

Mace, Alice E., ed. *The Birds Around Us.* San Francisco: Ortho Books, 1986.

National Geographic Society Field Guide to the Birds of North America. Washington: National Geographic Society, 1983.

Palmer, Ralph S., ed. *Handbook of North American Birds.* New Haven: Yale, 1988.

Parmer, Henry E., and Michael L. Bierly. *Birds of the Nashville Area*, third edition, 1975.

Perrins, Christopher M., and Alex L.A. Middleton, eds. *The Encyclopedia of Birds.* New York: Facts On File, 1985.

Peterson, Roger Tory. *A Field Guide to the Birds of Eastern and Central North America*. Peterson Field Guides. Boston: Houghton Mifflin, 1980.

————. *How To Know The Birds*. Boston: Houghton Mifflin, 1957.

Robbins, Chandler S., Bertel Bruun, and Herbert S. Zim. *Birds of North America. A Guide to Field Identification*. New York: Golden, 1966.

Robinson, John C. *An Annotated Checklist of the Birds of Tennessee*. Knoxville: University of Tennessee Press, 1990.

Saunders, Aretas A. *An Introduction to Bird Life for Bird Watchers*. New York: Dover, 1964.

Simonds, Calvin. *Private Lives of Garden Birds*. Emmaus, PA: Rodale, 1984.

Songbirds (All The World's Animals). New York: Torstar, 1985.

Stokes, Donald and Lillian. *The Bird Feeder Book*. Boston: Little, Brown, 1987.

Stokes, Donald W. *A Guide to the Behavior of Common Birds*. Boston: Little, Brown, 1979.

Terres, John K. *Songbirds in Your Garden*. New York: Crowell, 1953.

————. *The Audobon Society Encyclopedia of North American Birds*. New York: Knopf, 1980.

U.S. Department of Agriculture Forest Service Agriculture Handbook 688. *Forest and Rangeland Birds of the United States*. Washington: USDA, 1991.

van Tyne, Josselyn, and Andrew J. Berger. *Fundamentals of Ornithology*. New York: Dover, 1971.

Wallachinsky, David, and Irving Wallace. *The People's Almanac #2*. New York: Bantam, 1978.

Warton, Susan, ed. *An Illustrated Guide To Attracting Birds*. Menlo Park: Sunset, 1990.

Welty, Joel Carl. *The Life of Birds*. Philadelphia: Saunders, 1962.

Wetmore, Alexander. *Song and Garden Birds of North America*. Washington: National Geographic Society, 1964.

Zim, Herbert S., and Ira N. Gabrielson. *A Guide to Familiar American Birds*. New York: Golden, 1987.

IRIS, PASSIONFLOWER

Bailey, L. H. *How Plants Get Their Names*. New York: Macmillan, 1933.

————. *Manual of Cultivated Plants*. New York: Macmillan, 1951.

Campbell, Carlos C., William F. Hutson, and Aaron J. Sharp. *Great Smoky Mountains Wildflowers.* Knoxville: University of Tennessee Press, 1977.

Coffey, Timothy. *The History and Folklore of North American Wildflowers.* New York: Facts On File, 1993.

Haragan, Patricia Dalton. *Weeds of Kentucky and Adjacent States: A Field Guide.* Lexington: The University Press of Kentucky, 1991.

Healey, B. J. *A Gardener's Guide to Plant Names.* New York: Scribner's, 1972.

Hemmerly, Thomas E. *Wildflowers of the Central South.* Nashville: Vanderbilt University Press, 1990.

Hylander, Clarence J., and Edith Farrington Johnston. *The Macmillan Wildflower Book.* New York: The Macmillan Company, 1954.

Manchee, Fred B. *Our Heritage of Flowers.* New York: Holt, Rinehart and Winston, Inc, 1970.

Martin, Laura C. *Southern Wildflowers.* Atlanta: Longstreet, 1989.

Niering, William A., and Nancy C. Olmstead. *The Audobon Society Field Guide to North American Wildflowers.* New York: Knopf, 1979.

Novak, F. A. *The Pictorial Encyclopedia of Plants and Flowers.* New York: Crown, 1966.

Peterson, Roger Tory, and Margaret McKenny. *A Field Guide to Wildflowers, Northeastern and Northcentral North America.* The Peterson Field Guide Series. Boston: Houghton Mifflin, 1968.

Plowden, C. Chicheley. *A Manual of Plant Names.* New York: Philosophical Library, 1970.

Rickett, Harold William. *The New York Botanical Garden. Wild Flowers of The United States.* New York: McGraw-Hill.

Smith, Arlo I. *Guide to Wildflowers of the Mid-South.* Memphis: Memphis State University Press, 1979.

United States Dept. of Agriculture. *Common Weeds of the United States.* New York: Dover, 1971.

Usher, George. *A Dictionary of Botany.* London: Constable, 1966.

Venning, Frank D. *Wildflowers of North America: A Guide to Field Identificaton.* New York: Golden, 1984.

Wharton, Mary E., and Roger W. Barbour. *A Guide to The Wildflowers & Ferns of Kentucky.* Lexington: The University of Kentucky Press, 1971.

TULIP POPLAR TREE

Brockman, C. Frank. *Trees of North America*. New York: Golden, 1986.

Duncan, Wilbur H., and Maron B. Duncan. *Trees of the Southeastern United States*. Athens, GA: University of Georgia Press, 1988.

Edlin, Herbert L. *Trees and Man*. New York: Columbia University Press, 1976.

Graves, Arthur Harmount. *Illustrated Guide to Trees and Shrubs*. New York: Harper, 1956.

Little, Elbert L. *The Audobon Society Field Guide to North American Trees*. New York: Knopf, 1980.

Page, Jake. *Forest* (Planet Earth series). Alexandria, VA: Time-Life Books, 1983.

Peattie, Donald Culross. *A Natural History of Trees of Eastern and Central North America*. New York: Bonanza, 1966.

Petrides, George A. *A Field Guide to Trees and Shrubs*. (Peterson Field Guide series). Boston: Houghton Mifflin, 1986.

Phillips, Roger. *Trees of North America and Europe*. New York: Random House, 1978.

Simon and Schuster's Guide to Trees. New York: Simon and Schuster, 1978.

Symonds, George W. D. *The Tree Identification Book*. New York: Barrows, 1958.

Zim, Herbert S., and Alexander C. Martin. *A Guide to Familiar American Trees*. New York: Golden, 1987.

RACCOON

Alden, Peter. *Peterson First Guide. Mammals*. Boston: Houghton Mifflin, 1987.

Burt, William H., and Richard P. Grossenheider. *A Field Guide to the Mammals*. The Peterson Field Guide Series. Boston: Houghton Mifflin, 1964

Burton, Maurice. *Systematic Dictionary of Mammals of the World*. New York: Crowell, 1962.

Donald, David, ed. *The Encyclopedia of Mammals*. New York: Facts on File, 1984.

Ewer, R. F. *The Carnivores*. Ithaca: Cornell, 1973.

Godin, Alfred J. *Wild Mammals of New England*. Baltimore: Johns Hopkins, 1977.

Lowery, George H., Jr. *The Mammals of Louisiana and its Adjacent Waters*. Louisiana State University Press, 1974.

Nowak, Ronald M. *Walker's Mammals of the World*. Baltimore: Johns Hopkins, 1991.

Rue, Leonard Lee, III. *Pictorial Guide to the Mammals of North America*. New York: Crowell, 1967.

Schad, Wolfgang. *Man and Mammals*. New York: Waldorf, 1977.

Smith, Richard P. *Animal Tracks and Signs of North America*. Harrisburg: Stackpole, 1982.

Tanner, Ogden. *Beavers & Other Pond Dwellers*. (Wild, Wild World of Animals). Time-Life Films Inc, 1977.

van Gelder, Richard G. *Biology of Mammals*. New York: Scribner's, 1969.

LADYBUG, FIREFLY, HONEYBEE, ZEBRA SWALLOWTAIL

Arnett, Dr. Ross H., Jr., and Dr. Richard L. Jacques, Jr. *Simon & Schuster's Guide to Insects*. New York: Simon & Schuster, 1981.

Dines, Arthur M. *Honeybees From Close Up*. New York: Crowell, 1968.

Leahy, Christopher. Peterson First Guides: *Insects*. Boston: Houghton Mifflin, 1987.

Linsenmaier, Walter. *Insects of the World*. New York: McGraw-Hill, 1972.

Maeterlinck, Maurice. *The Life of the Bee*. New York: Dodd, Mead, 1958.

Milne, Lorus J., and Margery Milne. *Insect Worlds*. New York: Scribner's, 1980.

Nachtigall, Werner. *Insects In Flight*. New York: McGraw-Hill, 1968.

Newman, L. H. *Man and Insects*. London: Aldus, 1965.

O'Toole, Christopher, ed. *The Encyclopedia of Insects*. New York: Facts On File, 1986.

Stanek, V. J. *The Pictorial Encyclopedia of Insects*. New York: Hamlyn, 1969.

Sutherland, Louis. *The Life of the Queen Bee*. New York: Beechhurst, 1946.

Teale, Edwin Way. *The Golden Throng: A Book About Bees*. Sherborne: Alphabooks, 1968.

Tweedie, Michael. *Atlas of Insects*. New York: Day, 1974.

von Frisch, Karl. *Bees: Their Vision, Chemical Senses, and Language.* Ithaca, NY: Cornell University Press, 1971.
White, Richard E. *A Field Guide to the Beetles of North America.* The Peterson Field Guide Series. Boston: Houghton Mifflin, 1983.
Wigglesworth, V. B. *The Life of Insects.* New York: World, 1964.
Wilson, Edward O. *The Insect Societies.* Cambridge: Belknap, 1971.
Zim, Herbert S., and Clarence Cottam. *A Guide to Familiar American Insects.* New York: Golden, 1971.

CHANNEL CATFISH, LARGEMOUTH BASS

The Audobon Society Field Guide to North America Fishes, Whales, and Dolphins. New York: Knopf.
Carr, Archie, and Coleman J. Goin. *Guide to the Reptiles, Amphibians and Fresh-water Fishes of Florida.* Gainesville: Universtiy of Florida Press, 1955.
Crawford, Linda. *The Catfish Book.* Jackson: University Press of Mississippi, 1991.
Dozier, Thoims A. *Fishes of Lakes, Rivers & Oceans.* Wild, Wild World of Animals. Time-Life Films, 1979.
Eddy, Samuel. *How to Know the Freshwater Fishes.* Dubuque: Wm. C. Brown Co., 1957.
Herald, Earl S. *Fishes of North America.* New York: Doubleday, 1979.
LaMonte, Francesca. *North American Game Fishes.* New York: Doubleday, 1945.
Page, Lawrence M., and Brooks M. Burr. *A Field Guide to Freshwater Fishes,* The Peterson Field Guide Series. Boston: Houghton Mifflin, 1991.
Sterba, Gunther. *Freshwater Fishes of the World.* London: Vista, 1962.
Walden, Howard T. *Familiar Freshwater Fishes of America.* New York: Harper & Row, 1964.
Wheeler, Alwyne. *Fishes of the World: An Illustrated Dictionary.* New York: Macmillan, 1975.
Zim, Herbert S., and Hurst H. Shoemaker. *Fishes: A Guide to Fresh- and Salt-water Species.* New York: Golden, 1955.

LIMESTONE, AGATE

Hershey, Robert E. *Limestone and Dolomite Resources of Tennessee*. Bulletin 65. Tennessee Division of Geology, 1985.

MacFall, Russell P. *Gem Hunter's Guide*. New York: Crowell.

Pough, Frederick H. *A Field Guide to Rocks and Minerals*. Boston: Houghton Mifflin, 1951.

Rhodes, Frank H. T. *Geology*. New York: Golden, 1991.

Zim, Herbert S., and Paul R. Shaffer. *Rocks and Minerals*. New York: Golden, 1957.

Index

Debby Bowen

About The Author

Rob Simbeck was born and raised in Saint Marys, Pennsylvania, and is a graduate of the Creative Writing Program of Carnegie-Mellon University in Pittsburgh. He was city editor of *The Bradford* (Pa.) *Era*, then managing editor of *Music Connection* magazine in Los Angeles before moving to Nashville in 1983. He has written for *Guideposts, The Old Farmer's Almanac, Field & Stream, Birder's World, Wildbird*, conservation/wildlife magazines in 20 states, and many other publications. He lives in Hermitage.

ORDER FORM

Order a copy of *Tennessee State Symbols* as a gift for a relative, friend, or student. Just clip and mail the coupon below with a check or money order for the appropriate amount, and mail to:

Altheus Press
P.O. Box 25274
Nashville, TN 37202

In Tennessee:
   1 Book=$13.36 ($10.95+$1.50 shipping & handling+
      $.91 Tennessee sales tax)
   2 Books=$26.72 ($21.90+$3 S&H+$1.82 sales tax)
   3 or more Books=$10.69 per book ($8.95 per book+
      $1.00 S&H+$.74 sales tax)
Outside Tennessee:
   1 Book=$12.45 ($10.95+$1.50 shipping/handling)
   2 Books=$24.90 ($21.90+$3 S&H)
   3 or more Books=$9.95 per book ($8.95 per book+$1.00
      S&H)

Allow 4-6 weeks for delivery.

Yes. Send me _____ books. I am enclosing a check or money order for $_____.

Name_____

Address_____

City_____State_____Zip_____
